M000238245

Aunt Phil's Trunk Volume Three

Student Workbook

Bringing Alaska's history alive!

By
Laurel Downing Bill

Special credit and much appreciation to Nicole Cruz for her diligent efforts to create the best student workbook and teacher guide available for Alaska history studies.

Aunt Phil's Trunk LLC, Anchorage, Alaska
www.auntphilstrunk.com

International Standard Book Number 978-1-940479-34-7
Printed and bound in the United States of America.

First Printing 2017
First Printing Second Edition 2017
First Printing Third Edition 2018

Photo credits on the front cover, from top left: Native shaman with totem, Alaska State Library, Case and Draper Collection, ASL-P-39-782; Eskimo boy, Alaska State Library, Skinner Foundation, ASL-P44-11-002; Prospector, Alaska State Library, Skinner Foundation, ASL-P44-03-15; Athabascan woman, Anchorage Museum of History and Art, Crary–Henderson Collection, AMHA-b62-1-571; Gold miners, Alaska State Library, Harry T.Becker Collection, ASL-P67-052; Chilkoot Pass, Alaska State Library, Eric A. Hegg Collection, ASL-P124-04; Seal hunter, Alaska State Library, George A. Parks Collection, ASL-P240-210; Women mending boat, Alaska State Library, Rev. Samuel Spriggs Collection, ASL-P320-60; Students in class, Alaska State Library, Wickersham State Historical Site, ASL-P277-015-029.

TABLE OF CONTENTS

TABLE OF CONTENTS

Welcome to *Aunt Phil's Trunk Volume Three* Workbook for Students!

Read the chapters associated with each Unit. Then complete the lessons for that Unit to get a better understanding of Alaska's people and the events that helped shape Alaska's future.

I hope you enjoy your journey into Alaska's past from the years 1912 to 1935.

Laurel Downing Bill, author

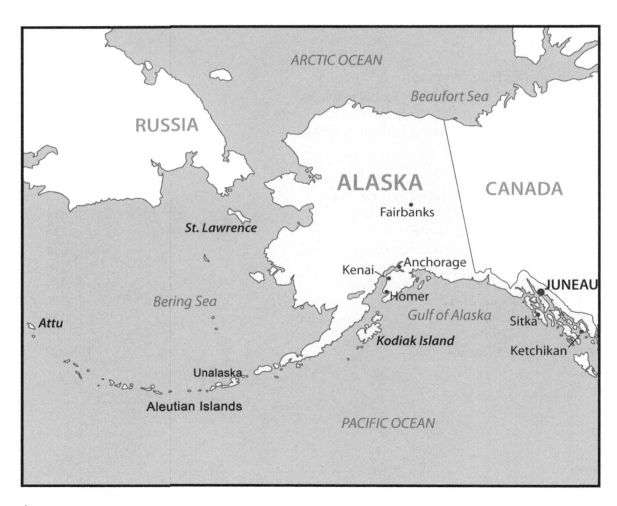

Instructions for using the Aunt Phil's Trunk Alaska History Curriculum

The *Aunt Phil's Trunk* Alaska History Curriculum is designed to be used in grades 4-8. High school students can use this curriculum, also, by taking advantage of the essay and enrichment activities throughout the book. The next few pages give further instruction on how to use this curriculum with middle school students, high school students and in classroom settings.

This curriculum can be taught in multiple grade levels by having your older students complete all reading, study guide work and enrichment activities independently. Students of all grade levels can participate in daily oral review by playing games like Jeopardy or Around the World.

This curriculum was developed so that students not only learn about Alaska's past, but they will have fun in the process. After every few lessons, they can test their knowledge through word scramble, word search and crossword puzzles.

Notes for parents with younger students:

Enrichment Activities occasionally direct your child to watch educational videos on YouTube.com or link to other Websites to learn more about the topic that they are reading about in the lesson. You may want to supervise younger children while they are using the Internet to be sure that they do not click on any inappropriate content. This also provides a good opportunity to discuss Internet safety with your child/children.

How to use this workbook at home

Aunt Phil's Trunk Alaska History Curriculum is designed to be used in grades 4-8. High school students can use this curriculum, also, by taking advantage of the essay and enrichment activities throughout the book. The next page gives further instruction on how to use this curriculum with high school students.

This curriculum can be taught in multiple grade levels by having your older students complete all reading, study guide work and enrichment activities independently. Students of all grade levels can participate in daily oral review by playing games like Jeopardy or Around the World.

For Middle School Students:

1. **Facts to Know:** Read this section in the study guide with your student(s) before reading the chapter to get familiar with new terms that they will encounter in the reading.

2. **Read the chapter:** Read one chapter aloud to your student(s) or have them read it aloud to you. Older students may want to read independently.

3. **Comprehension Questions:** Younger students may answer the comprehension questions orally or write down their answers in the study guide. Use these questions to test your student(s) comprehension of the chapter. Older students should answer all questions in written form.

4. **Discussion Questions:** Have your student(s) answer these questions in a few sentences orally. Come up with follow-up questions to test your student(s) understanding of the material. Older students may answer discussion questions in written essay form.

5. **Map Work:** Some chapters will contain a map activity for your student(s) to learn more about the geography of the region that they are learning about.

6. **Enrichment and Online References:** (Optional) Assign enrichment activities as you see fit. Many of the online references are from the Alaska Humanities Forum website (http://www.akhistorycourse.org). We highly recommend this website for additional information, project ideas, etc.

7. **Unit Review:** At the end of a unit, your student will complete Unit Review questions and word puzzles in the study guide. Students should review all the chapters in the unit before completing the review. Parents may want to assist younger students with the word puzzles.

8. **Unit Test:** (Optional) There is an optional test that you can administer to your student(s) after they have completed all the unit work.

How to use this workbook for high school

1. **Facts to Know:** Your student(s) should read this section in the study guide before reading the chapter to get familiar with new terms that they will encounter.

2. **Read the chapter:** Your student(s) can read aloud or independently.

3. **Comprehension Questions:** Use these questions to test your student(s) comprehension of the chapter. Have your high schoolers write out their answers in complete sentences.

4. **Discussion Questions:** Have your student(s) answer these questions in a few sentences orally or write out their answer in essay form.

5. **Map Work:** Some chapters will contain a map activity for your student(s) to learn more about the geography of the region that they are learning about.

6. **Enrichment and Online References:** Once your high schooler has completed all the reading and study guide material for the chapter, assign additional reading from the enrichment material using the online links or book lists. Encourage your student(s) to explore topics of interest to them.

Many of the online references are from the Alaska Humanities Forum website. We highly recommend this website for additional information, project ideas, etc.

7. **Unit Review:** At the end of a unit, your student will complete Unit Review questions and word puzzles in their study guide. Students should review all the chapters in the unit before completing the review.

8. **Unit Test:** (Optional) There is an optional test that you can administer to your student(s) after they have completed all the unit work.

9. **Oral Presentation:** (Optional) Assign a 5-minute oral presentation on any topic in the reading. Encourage your student(s) to utilize the additional books and online resources to supplement the information in the textbook. Set aside a classroom day for your student(s) to share their presentations.

10. **Historical Inquiry Project:** Your student(s) will choose a topic from the reading to learn more about and explore that topic through library visits, museum trips, visiting historical sites, etc.

Visit https://www.nhd.org/how-enter-contest for detailed information on how to put together a historical inquiry project. You may even want to have your students enter the national contest.

How to use this workbook in the classroom

Aunt Phil's Trunk Alaska History Curriculum was created for homeschooling families, but it also can work well in a co-op or classroom setting. Here are some suggestions on how to use this curriculum in a classroom setting. Use what works best for your classroom.

1. **Facts to Know:** The teacher introduces students to the Facts to Know to familiarize the students with terms that they will encounter in the chapter.

2. **Read the chapter:** The teacher can read the chapter aloud while the students follow along in the book. Students also may take turns reading aloud.

3. **Comprehension Questions:** The teacher uses these questions to test the students' comprehension of the chapter. Students should write out the answers in their study guide and the teacher can review the answers with the students in class.

4. **Discussion Questions:** The teacher chooses a few students to answer these questions orally during class. Alternatively, teachers can assign these questions to be completed in essay form individually and answers can be shared during class.

5. **Map Work:** Some chapters will contain a map activity for your students to learn more about the geography of the region that they are learning about. Have your students complete the activity independently.

6. **Enrichment and Online References:** Assign enrichment activities as you see fit.

7. **Daily Review:** Students should review the material for the current unit daily. You can do this by asking review questions orally. Playing review games like Jeopardy or Around the World is a fun way to get your students excited about the material.

8. **Unit Review:** At the end of a unit, your student will complete Unit Review questions and word puzzles in the study guide. Have students review all the unit chapters before completing.

9. **Unit Test:** (Optional) There is an optional test that you can administer to your students after they have completed all the unit work.

10. **Oral Presentation:** (Optional) Assign a 5-minute oral presentation on any topic in the reading. Encourage your students to utilize the additional books and online resources to supplement the information in the textbook. Set aside a classroom day for students to share their presentations.

11. **Historical Inquiry Project:** Your student(s) will choose a topic from the reading to learn more about and explore that topic through library visits, museum trips, visiting historical sites, etc.

Visit https://www.nhd.org/how-enter-contest for detailed information on how to put together a historical inquiry project. You may even want to have your students enter the national contest.

How to grade the assignments

Our rubric grids are designed to make it easy for you to grade your students' essays, oral presentations and enrichment activities. Encourage your students to look at the rubric grid before completing an assignment as a reminder of what an exemplary assignment should include.

You can mark grades for review questions, essay tests and extra credit assignments on the last page of each unit in the student workbook. Use these pages as a tool to help your students track their progress and improve their assignment grades.

Unit Review Questions

Students are given one point for each correct review and fill-in-the-blank question. Mark these points on the last page of each unit in the student workbook.

Essay Test Questions

Students will complete two or more essay questions at the end of each unit. These questions are designed to test your students' knowledge about the key topics of each unit. You can give a student up to 20 points for each essay.

Students are graded on a scale of 1-5 in four categories:

1) Understanding the topic
2) Answering all questions completely and accurately
3) Neatness and organization
4) Grammar, spelling and punctuation

Use the essay rubric grid on page 11 as a guide to give up to 5 points in each category for every essay. Mark these points for each essay on the last page of each Unit Review in the student workbook.

Word Puzzles

Word puzzles that appear at the end of the Unit Reviews count for 5 points, or you can give partial points if the student does not fill in the puzzle completely. Mark these points under the extra category on the last page of each Unit Review in the student workbook.

Enrichment Activities

Most lessons contain an enrichment activity for further research and interaction with the information in the lesson. You can make these optional or assign every activity as part of the lesson. You can use the provided rubric on page 12 to give up to 5 points for each assignment. Mark these points under the extra category on the last page of each Unit Review in the student workbook.

Oral Presentations

You have the option of assigning oral presentations on any topic from the unit as extra credit. If you choose to assign oral presentations, you can use the provided rubric to grade your student on content and presentation skills. Discuss what presentation skills you will be grading your student on before each presentation day.

Some examples of presentation skills you can grade on include:

- Eye contact with the audience
- Proper speaking volume
- Using correct posture
- Speaking clearly

Use the oral presentation rubric grid on page 12 as a guide to give up to 10 points. Mark these points under the extra category on the last page of each Unit Review in the student workbook.

Rubric for Essay Questions

	Beginning 1	Needs Improvement 2	Acceptable 3	Accomplished 4	Exemplary 5
Demonstrates Understanding of the topic	Student's work shows incomplete understanding of the topic	Student's work shows slight understanding of the topic	Student's work shows a basic understanding of the topic	Student's work shows complete understanding of the topic	Student's work demonstrates strong insight about the topic
Answered questions completely and accurately	Student's work did not address all of the questions	Student answered all of the questions with some accuracy	Student answered all questions with close to 100% accuracy	Student answered all questions with 100% accuracy	Student goes beyond the questions to demonstrate knowledge of the topic
Essay is neat and well organized	Student's work is sloppy and unorganized	Student's work is somewhat neat and organized	Student's essay is neat and somewhat organized	Student's work is well organized and neat	Student demonstrates extra care in organizing the essay and making it neat
Essay contains good grammar and spelling	Student's work is poorly written and hard to understand	Student's work contains some grammar, spelling and punctuation mistakes, but not enough to impede understanding	Student's work contains only 1 or 2 grammar, spelling or punctuation errors	Student's work contains no grammar, spelling or punctuation errors	Student's work is extremely well-written

Rubric for Oral Presentations

	Beginning 1	Needs Improvement 2	Acceptable 3	Accomplished 4	Exemplary 5
Preparation	Student did not prepare for the presentation	Student was somewhat prepared for the presentation	Student was prepared for the presentation and addressed the topic	Student was well-prepared for the presentation and addressed important points about the topic	Student prepared an excellent presentation that exhibited creativity and originality
Presentation Skills	Student demonstrated poor presentation skills (no eye contact, low volume, appears disinterested in the topic)	Student made some effort to demonstrate presentation skills (eye contact, spoke clearly, engaged audience, etc.)	Student demonstrated acceptable presentation skills (eye contact, spoke clearly, engaged audience, etc.)	Student demonstrated good presentation skills (eye contact, spoke clearly, engaged audience, etc.)	Student demonstrated strong presentation skills (eye contact, spoke clearly, engaged audience, etc.)

Rubric for Enrichment Activities

Beginning 1	Needs Improvement 2	Acceptable 3	Accomplished 4	Exemplary 5
Student's work is incomplete or inaccurate	Student's work is complete and somewhat inaccurate	Student completed the assignment with accuracy	Student's work is accurate, complete, neat and well-organized	Student demonstrates exceptional creativity or originality

UNIT 1: EARLY COOK INLET

LESSON 1: COOK INLET TIMELINE

FACTS TO KNOW

Cook Inlet – Area of southcentral Alaska that stretches 180 miles from the Gulf of Alaska to Anchorage

Dena'ina – Native people of the Cook Inlet area (also called Tanaina)

Alaska Homestead Law – Provided land for settlers in Alaska

COMPREHENSION QUESTIONS

1) When was the earliest-known human habitation of the Cook Inlet area? What people group lived there? What people group displaced them? _____

_____

_____

_____

2) How did the Cook Inlet receive its name? _____

_____

_____

3) Why did the Dena'ina population in the upper inlet plummet by half between 1835-1845? _____

_____

_____

4) Due to mounting diplomatic problems in Europe and Asia, the _____ sold Alaska to the _____ for $7.2 million in 1867. When _____ discovered gold around _____ in 1888 and _____ in 1893, thousands of hopeful _____ streamed into Cook Inlet.

5) What was the purpose of the Alaska Homestead Law in 1898? What revisions were made in 1903 and 1912? _____

_____

_____

_____

6) Congress passed the _____

that made Alaska a U. S. territory.

DISCUSSION QUESTION

(Discuss this question with your teacher or write your answer in essay form below. Use additional paper if necessary.)

Briefly summarize the history of Cook Inlet from early human habitation to 1914.

_____
_____
_____
_____
_____
_____
_____
_____
_____
_____
_____
_____
_____
_____
_____
_____
_____
_____
_____

ENRICHMENT ACTIVITY

Using Chapter 1, create a Cook Inlet timeline of events. Begin with the first wave of early human habitation in the inlet, and then end with the 1914 Alaska Railroad Act.

LEARN MORE

The Cook Inlet Collection: Two Hundred Years of Selected Alaskan History, Morgan Sherwood. Anchorage: Alaska Northwest Publishing Company, 1974.

UNIT 1: EARLY COOK INLET

LESSON 2: RAILROAD MAKES HEADLINES

FACTS TO KNOW

Seward – A city in the Kenai Peninsula named for U.S. Secretary of State William H. Seward

John Ballaine – Founder of the city of Seward who believed the town would be the metropolis of a great territory

Alaska Railroad Act – Allowed the president to locate, construct and operate a railroad that would unite the Pacific Ocean with the navigable waters of Interior Alaska

COMPREHENSION QUESTIONS

1) What newspaper headline "resurrected" the town of Seward? Why was this news so important to the residents of Seward? _____

_____

_____

_____

2) How did this news change the economy of Seward? _____

_____

_____

_____

3) What obstacles delayed the building of the railroad? What happened to John Ballaine's Alaska Central Railroad company? _____

_____

_____

_____

_____

4) How did Judge James Wickersham play a part in getting the railroad built?

_____

_____

_____

_____

5) Why did the government eventually change their plans to make the railroad headquarters in Seward? What area was chosen as the headquarters? _____

_____

_____

_____

_____

DISCUSSION QUESTION

(Discuss this question with your teacher or write your answer in essay form below. Use additional paper if necessary.)

What do you think about the poem by Pat P. Cotter on Pages 24 and 25?

_____

_____

_____

_____

_____

_____

_____

_____

_____

_____

_____

_____

_____

ENRICHMENT ACTIVITY

Learn more about the Alaska railroad route by visiting https://www.alaskarailroad.com/ride-a-train/route-map
See how many cities you recognize from your lesson on the route map.

LEARN MORE

Read more about Alaska railroad construction by visiting http://www.akhistorycourse.org/southcentral-alaska/1915-1930-the-railroad-years

UNIT 1: EARLY COOK INLET

LESSON 3: KNIK WITHERS

FACTS TO KNOW

Knik – Small trading town in Cook Inlet

Alaska Engineering Commission – A group of three men (William C. Edes, Lt. Frederick Mears and Thomas Riggs) were appointed to scout out the railway route

COMPREHENSION QUESTIONS

1) What industry did Knik rely upon beginning in 1834? _____

_____

_____

2) How did activities in other parts of Alaska bring life into the settlement of Knik? (Hint: gold rush and Iditarod Trail) _____

_____

_____

_____

3) What event caused Knik to become the major trading center for gold and coal?

_____

_____

_____

_____

4) How did the Alaska Railroad Act of 1914 cause Knik to become a ghost town?

_____

_____

_____

_____

DISCUSSION QUESTION

(Discuss this question with your teacher or write your answer in essay form below. Use additional paper if necessary.)

Why were the residents of Knik angry at the government?

_____
_____
_____
_____
_____
_____
_____
_____
_____
_____
_____
_____
_____
_____
_____
_____
_____

LEARN MORE

Read more about the ups and downs of the building of the Alaska railroad by visiting http://www.akhistorycourse.org/americas-territory/alaskas-heritage/chapter-4-11-railroad-transportation

TIME TO REVIEW

Review Chapters 1-3 of your book before moving on to the Unit Review. See how many questions you can answer without looking at your book.

Early Cook Inlet Landmarks
Word Search Puzzle
Find the words listed below

```
T Y E P X X D V V L A R         X S W D P J
M         I R P Y O V I           C L K C
R         X A R K Y N W W           Q M
E         T W V W A O T U     J O   I V
W         A E E H B I R R   Q X     S S
D H K A M L S T U N T B H B I T P R K V V I G Y
D A A K T K R I M O A M Z D K I H C L I N I N P J Y
Z R N S B E D F D I T S Y D L H F P W A S I L L A L
A S C U V E J O N T S A T G I R D W O O D V B B H B
I Z H N T T E L U C A L T X E M M A H A R G T R O P
V W O A U N W I A E N G E P X W O L L I W J F M I
O E R T R A A S E R T U L D Z O E J B O P L C W D
D V A A N A H A X R I O N H S S A P E G A T R O P
L U G M A B S K G U S D I W K E E R C P I H S L T P
E Y E S G D X K W S U E K B C L R I U S T Y O N E K M
S K N K A H O P E E S P O I E S I R N U S B N D F F S D
L I L S I E Y A A R V A O W L I A N E K L U T N A E V Y S
    S N N N U   K P C C K   Z J M K F   A I H C E
    N T K     X S M     B A S     H L X
```

TURNAGAIN	KNIK	COOK INLET
KASILOF	KENAI	TYONEK
SELDOVIA	NINILCHIK	EKLUTNA
PORT GRAHAM	SUSITNA STATION	PORTAGE PASS
CAPE DOUGLAS	TALKEETNA	MATANUSKA
WASILLA	ANCHORAGE	SHIP CREEK
SUNRISE	HOPE	GIRDWOOD
SEWARD	RESURRECTION BAY	WILLOW

UNIT 1: EARLY COOK INLET

REVIEW LESSONS 1-3

Write down what you remember about:

Cook Inlet _____

_____

Dena'ina _____

_____

Alaska Homestead Law _____

_____

Seward _____

_____

John Ballaine _____

_____

Alaska Railroad Act _____

_____

Knik _____

_____

George W. Palmer _____

_____

Fill in the blanks:

1) _____ entered Cook Inlet through mountain passes to the west as early as _____ and as late as 1650 A.D., displacing the _____. The _____, also called _____, adapted the Alutiiq peoples' knowledge of living in a coastal region, such as using _____ for saltwater fishing, and subsisted entirely on the _____.

2) When _____ discovered gold around _____ in 1888 and _____ Creek in 1893, thousands of hopeful miners streamed into Cook Inlet. Stampeders, who had to travel to St. _____ or _____ to get to the rich diggings in the Yukon, began demanding an all-American route be blazed. After many years of surveying routes, the government deemed that a _____ would be a good mode of transportation.

3) Congress extended homesteading to Alaska under the _____ Law in _____. It differed from the original provisions of the 1862 law, which covered the rest of the _____, in that a homesteader was limited to _____ and limited entry to surveyed land.

4) 'EXTRA! EXTRA!' An extra in a small town like _____ is a sensation, but more sensational was the news. The U. S. government had chosen _____ as the saltwater _____ for its proposed government _____.

5) Boatloads of men arrived from the states seeking work on the new _____, which was to be built from the deepwater port of _____ to Alaska's _____ where abundant resources like _____ and _____ awaited transportation to the coast.

6) President _____ signed the _____ into law in 1914 and Secretary of Interior Franklin Lane appointed three men, geologist _____ and experienced railroad builders _____ and _____, to the Alaska Engineering Commission.

7) Residents of _____ weren't happy when the _____ was established at _____ instead of their town. The reason for the change, officials said, was because the government was confronted with legal obstructions and _____ in its purchase of the Alaska Northern and surrounding property.

8) The residents of _____, which had become a thriving _____ center during the late 1890s, first started trading with white men when the _____ established a mission there in 1834.

9) After the American purchase of Alaska, _____ opened a store there in the 1880s called _____. It relied upon the local _____.

10) The _____ of 1914 spelled the end of Knik. The route chosen to connect _____ to the Matanuska coalfields and on to _____ bypassed the community on _____ Arm, and its residents eventually moved to either _____ or the railroad camp on Ship Creek called _____.

Alaska Central Railway, seen above in 1906, was the first railroad going out of Seward. By 1908 it had gone bankrupt. Next came Alaska Northern, seen below in 1910. Alaska Northern became part of the Alaska Railroad in 1914.

UNIT 1: EARLY COOK INLET

UNIT TEST

Choose *two* of the following questions to answer in paragraph form. Use as much detail as possible to completely answer the question. Use extra paper in back of the book if needed.

1) Describe three important events that occurred in the timeline of Cook Inlet history from 3000 B.C. to 1914. Why were these events important?

2) What sleepy town received good news in the summer of 1914? What good news did this town receive? In what ways did this news immediately impact the town? How did the government ultimately let down this town?

3) What industries did the town of Knik rely upon beginning in 1834? How did the Alaska Railroad Act affect the town of Knik?

UNIT 1: EARLY COOK INLET

Review Questions .... (possible 8 pts.)
Fill-the-Blanks .... (possible 10 pts.)

Unit Test

Essay 1
Demonstrates understanding of the topic .... (possible 5 pts.)
Answered the questions completely and accurately .... (possible 5 pts.)
Composition is neat .... (possible 5 pts.)
Grammar and Spelling .... (possible 5 pts.)

Essay 2
Demonstrates understanding of the topic .... (possible 5 pts.)
Answered the questions completely and accurately .... (possible 5 pts.)
Composition is neat .... (possible 5 pts.)
Grammar and Spelling .... (possible 5 pts.)

Subtotal Points .... **(possible 58 pts.)**

Extra Credit
Word Puzzle .... (5 pt. per completed puzzle)
Complete an Enrichment Activity .... (possible 5 pts.)
Oral presentation .... (possible 10 pts.)

Total Extra Credit ....

Total Unit Points ....

GRADE CHART

A   53-58+ points

B   47-52 points

C   41-46 points

D   35-40 points

UNIT 2: EARLY RAILROAD DAYS

LESSON 4: RAILROAD BIRTHS ANCHORAGE

FACTS TO KNOW

Anchorage – Cook Inlet city that was chosen as the headquarters of the Alaska Railroad

Woodrow Wilson – U.S. president who pushed to build the Alaska Railroad in 1914

COMPREHENSION QUESTIONS

1) The _____ authorized the president to locate, construct, and operate a railroad that would unite the _____ with the navigable waters of _____. The railroad could not exceed _____ miles in length and could not cost more than $_____.

2) Why did President Woodrow Wilson create the Alaska Railroad Commission? Who did he appoint to this group? _____

_____

_____

_____

_____

3) What two routes did the Alaska Railroad Commission study? _____

_____

_____

_____

_____

4) Which route was chosen after the commission completed their study? _____

_____

_____

_____

_____

5) According to a 1921 report to the Secretary of Interior, how much did it cost per mile to build the railroad? What supplies were needed to build the railroad? From where did the supplies come? _____

_____

_____

_____

_____

DISCUSSION QUESTION

(Discuss this question with your teacher or write your answer in essay form below. Use additional paper if necessary.)

Describe some of the challenges that residents of early Anchorage faced.

_____

_____

_____

_____

_____

_____

_____

_____

_____

_____

_____

_____

_____

_____

_____

_____

LEARN MORE

Read more about the reconnaissance survey for the Alaska railroad by visiting
http://content.lib.washington.edu/alaskawcanadaweb/kuskokwim.html

MAP ACTIVITY

The Alaska Railroad Commission studied two routes to Alaska's Interior– one from Cordova and one from Seward – before choosing the Susitna route. Fill in the boxes for places that sit along those routes: 1) Cordova 2) Childs Glacier 3) Seward 4) Portage/ Whittier 5) Anchorage 6) Wasilla 7)Talkeetna 8) Denali 9) Fairbanks

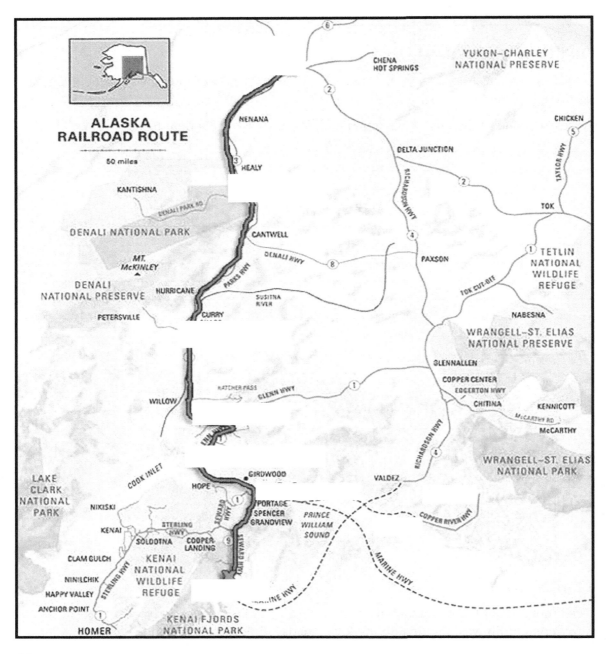

UNIT 2: EARLY RAILROAD DAYS

LESSON 5: SHIP CREEK BLOSSOMS

FACTS TO KNOW

Ship Creek – A creek located between Seward and Fairbanks
Lot auction – Process of buying and selling a lot of land going to the highest bidder
World War I – Global war originating in Europe that lasted from 1914 to 1918

COMPREHENSION QUESTIONS

1) Why did the Alaska Engineering Commission recommend Ship Creek as the headquarters for the government railroad? _____

_____

_____

_____

_____

2) How did George C. Hazelet describe Ship Creek to the *Cordova Daily Times* in 1915?

_____

_____

_____

_____

_____

3) What were living conditions like in the early days at Ship Creek? _____

_____

_____

_____

_____

4) What were the results of the first town lot auction in Ship Creek in July 1915? _____

_____

_____

_____

_____

5) How did the area known as Ship Creek receive the name Anchorage? _____

_____

_____

_____

6) Describe the first public school in Anchorage. _____

_____

_____

_____

7) What important historical event caused the Alaska Railroad workforce to go from more than 5,600 to 2,800 by 1918? Why? _____

_____

_____

_____

DISCUSSION QUESTION

(Discuss this question with your teacher or write your answer in essay form below. Use additional paper if necessary.)

How did the government railroad lead to the development of a new city called Anchorage?

_____

_____

_____

_____

_____

_____

_____

_____

ENRICHMENT ACTIVITY

Imagine that you are one of the thousands of people that traveled to Ship Creek in order to work on the railroad. Write a letter to your friend back home about your adventure. What is the town like? What are your living conditions like? What is the work like?

LEARN MORE

Watch this short YouTube video about the building of the Alaska Railroad:
https://www.youtube.com/watch?v=c5U9o3E-XLI

UNIT 2: EARLY RAILROAD DAYS

LESSON 6: GOLDEN SPIKE MYSTERY

FACTS TO KNOW

Railroad spike – Large nails used to hold the rails in place

Warren G. Harding – The first U.S. president to visit Alaska

Metlakatla – First stop on U.S Predient Warren G. Harding's trip to Alaska where he was welcomed by Tsimshian people with traditional music and dancing

Ketchikan – Southeast Alaska city that greeted President Harding and his party with a brass band

COMPREHENSION QUESTIONS

1) When was the railroad completed? What was done to commemorate the occasion?

_____

_____

_____

_____

2) According to Secretary of Commerce Herbert C. Hoover, how did President Warren Harding feel about traveling to Alaska in 1923? _____

_____

_____

_____

3) What did President Harding do on July 15, 1923, to complete the construction of the Alaska railroad? _____

_____

_____

_____

4) What did President Harding say about Alaska when he reached Seattle? How did he become ill at the end of his trip? _____

_____

_____

_____

_____

31

5) President Warren Harding died on Aug. 2, 1923, less than three weeks after he drove the golden spike into the last piece of track for the Alaska Railroad. What are some theories about his cause of death? _____

_____

_____

_____

_____

DISCUSSION QUESTION

(Discuss this question with your teacher or write your answer in essay form below. Use additional paper if necessary.)

Explain the mystery of the golden spike.

_____

_____

_____

_____

_____

_____

_____

_____

_____

_____

_____

_____

_____

_____

_____

_____

LEARN MORE

Read more about the 29th U.S. president by visiting https://www.whitehouse.gov/1600/presidents/warrenharding

TIME TO REVIEW

Review Chapters 4-6 of your book before moving on the Unit Review. See how many questions you can answer without looking at your book.

Many Alaska children were excited to see U.S. President Warren
G. Harding in July 1923, the first president to visit Alaska.

Alaska Railroad

Crossword Puzzle

Read Across and Down clues and fill in blank boxes that match numbers on the clues

Across

3 Goods transported in railroad cars

5 This was a huge problem on dirt streets along Ship Creek in 1915

6 Alaska Engineering Commission overlooked this in the new town along Ship Creek

11 Pacific Coast port where building materials and supplies began journey to build Alaska Railroad

12 Railroad started in 1902 & went bankrupt 1908

15 Type of engine that powered Alaska Railroad trains in early 1900s

19 Route chosen to lay tracks for the Alaska Railroad

21 Area just north of Ship Creek that had mining and grazing potential

23 Supply center whose Indian name means "fire"

26 Name of last car in a railroad train

29 Name for person who labors building a railroad

31 Superintendent of lot sales in Ship Creek

34 Name of deep-water bay at Seward

35 Fourth Avenue of Anchorage was laid out for this purpose

Across (Continued)

36 Name of railroad that took over Seward's railroad in 1910

39 Structure used to carry railroad across a river or other obstacle

41 This sprang up on the north bank of Ship Creek when 2,000 people arrived in 1915

43 A continuous line of rails for a railroad

46 First, Second and Third avenues of Anchorage were set aside for this purpose

47 Name of second school that opened in Anchorage in December 1917

48 First car that provides power to pull the trail

49 U.S. president who pounded last spike in Alaska Railroad to signify its completion 1923

52 A large nail that secures railway rails to the ties

53 A yellow ore found abundantly in Alaska that needed to be transported to Seward

55 Valley just north of Ship Creek that had potential to develop into a farming community

56 Ship that carried Lt. Frederick Mears to Alaska in late April 1915

Down

1 Secretary of Interior in 1914

2 U.S. President who signed the Alaska Railroad Act in 1914

4 Geologist for Alaska Railroad

7 The building of the railroad

8 Name for what became Anchorage that actually won the most votes during an election on Aug. 2, 1915

9 Member of the Alaska Engineering Commission

10 Town chosen as the end of the Alaska Railroad

13 Commission created in 1914 to build Alaska Railroad

14 The farthest point reached in constructing a railroad

16 Man who wanted to name town after Secretary of State William H. Seward

(Down Continued)

17 An extensive area containing a number of coal deposits

18 Author of the "Wandering Boy"

20 The area of land alongside a coast

21 Judge who urged Congress to pass legislation to build an Alaska railroad

22 Major event that pulled workers away from building the Alaska Railroad in 1918

24 Country from which much of the machinery used to build the Alaska Railroad originated

25 The first cabin on Ship Creek was built by this man

27 Name of U. S. transport that brought a U.S. president to Alaska in 1923

28 Man who wrote the poem "The Unholy Trinity"

30 A structure extending alongshore or out from the shore into a body of water

Alaska Railroad
Crossword Puzzle Key

(Down Continued)

32 Member of the Alaska Engineering Commission
33 First butcher in Anchorage
37 Started one of the first dry goods businesses in Anchorage
38 Alaska's Territorial governor at the time that the Alaska Railroad began construction
42 Indians who had fish sites and smokehouses around Ship Creek in 1914
44 The chimney of a locomotive
45 Headquarters for the U.S. government's railroad project
50 Spacing of rails on a railway track
51 Term for end point of Alaska Railroad
54 Name of railroad car that has special comfort and sleeping berths

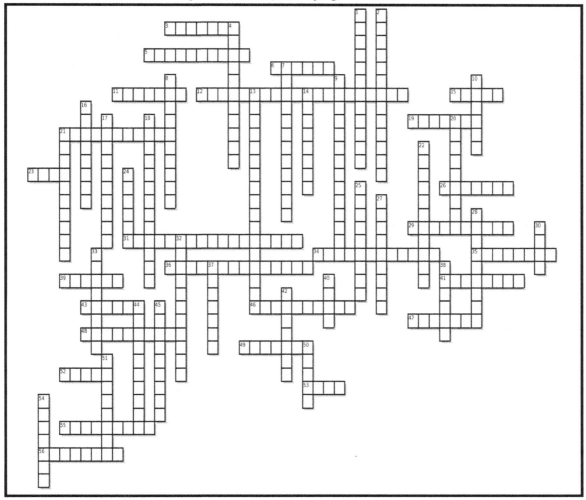

UNIT 2: EARLY RAILROAD DAYS

REVIEW LESSONS 4-6

Write down what you remember about:

Anchorage _____

_____

President Woodrow Wilson _____

_____

Ship Creek _____

_____

Lot auction _____

_____

World War I _____

_____

Railroad spike _____

_____

President Warren G. Harding _____

_____

Metlakatla _____

_____

Ketchikan _____

_____

Fill in the blanks:

1) At first the _____, which was created in 1914 and developed the railroad, only saw the site at _____ as a major construction camp and terminal point along a route to link Seward with Interior Alaska.

2) Ship Creek's central location to the entire _____, and skyrocketing land prices in the deepwater port of _____, caused the commission to change its mind in 1915 and make _____ its headquarters.

3) While studying routes, the _____ came upon _____, which was centrally located between _____ and _____. It had a protected _____ that could be dredged and a large amount of _____ on which a construction camp could be built.

4) Upon hearing of the new construction camp in Cook Inlet, hoards of men and women poured into _____ hoping to snag jobs building _____. When Frederick Mears stepped off the steamer *Mariposa* in late April 1915, he saw hundreds of _____ and _____ housing those awaiting work.

5) One observer gave the *Cordova Daily Times* an account of what he saw on a trip to the _____ camp. "I found the largest _____ I ever saw," George C. Hazelet said in an interview on June 29, 1915. "From 2,000 to 2,500 people are fed, housed, and their wants, in a way, taken care of in _____, all located on the government _____ ground."

6) Living conditions were less than ideal as more and more _____ arrived along the creek. With no _____, and Cook Inlet tides providing the only means of _____ , the Alaska Engineering Commission surgeon warned that the new settlement's _____ soon would become contaminated.

7) The first _____ on July 10, 1915, opened with enthusiastic bidding. At its conclusion, the _____ Office had auctioned _____ for about $_____. Local merchants had paid more for _____ along _____ Avenue than anywhere else in town.

8) The _____ Office arbitrarily named the new Alaska settlement at Ship Creek _____.

9) To commemorate the end of construction on the Alaska Railroad, _____ traveled to Alaska to _____. He was the first _____ to visit the territory.

10) President _____ hammered a symbolic _____ into the railroad track at _____ on _____. The $600 _____ then was replaced with an _____ one to finish the track.

11) President Harding began experiencing _____ after eating crab drenched in butter. _____ was suspected. The President became more ill as he traveled by train to San Francisco. Harding, 57, _____ on Aug. 2, less than three weeks after he _____ into the last piece of track for the _____.

Possible Names for Ship Creek Town in Forest
Word Search Puzzle
Find the words listed below

```
          X  B
          G  Y
       U  V  B  P
       Q  T  F  N
    N  U  M  F  U  Q
    W  B  R  P  I  Z
 T  I  W  D  G  F  N  Z
 Z  N  C  X  B  P  M  V
 Z  X  A  A  K  I  Z  D  Q  E
 L  N  L  D  H  P  B  H  G  L
 Y  L  K  A  T  I  I  X  A  B  S  L
 H  D  U  S  I  A  D  R  N  B  D  F
 K  E  K  T  K  X  L  O  F  R  K  R  S  L
 K  R  K  E  A  R  H  C  O  D  O  X  K  Z
 X  Y  C  J  O  E  C  H  W  A  L  O  D  V  E  P
 M  M  T  Y  D  N  R  N  U  A  L  T  D  N  H  S
 E  F  L  E  A  A  J  S  C  R  H  V  R  H  H  P  G  P
 X  A  N  E  L  H  V  W  Y  P  L  A  N  I  M  R  E  T
 E  N  T  T  A  S  I  Z  G  T  A  I  G  K  T  U  P  J  O  G
 E  I  S  S  U  L  Z  O  Z  I  D  V  H  I  S  N  F  R  T  A
 U  H  E  K  F  L  T  M  G  F  C  B  F  K  S  A  U  M  F  N  F  F
 W  M  A  B  E  S  O  W  T  O  W  I  C  Z  N  Y  N  N  F  F  V  J
 J  O  C  T  R  Y  F  W  E  O  R  O  Y  B  G  B  E  G  Z  A  K  A  T  H
 H  I  P  L  V  Q  R  I  V  A  G  R  A  D  X  D  F  J  A  P  T  C  J  X
 F  T  M  I  L  A  Q  K  Y  A  P  J  D  W  Q  V  I  J  K  I  O  F  A  I  G  E
 Y  P  B  O  F  L  L  A  M  B  Y  E  O  E  P  J  K  I  N  K  W  E  N  M  Z  D
          J  O  T  L
          J  W  A  F
          R  V  G  Q
```

MATANUSKA	TERMINAL	NEW KNIK
ALASKA CITY	SHIP CREEK	WOODROW CITY
GATEWAY	WINALASKA	HOMESTEAD
LANE	WHITNEY	BROWNSVILLE
ANCHORAGE		

UNIT 2: EARLY RAILROAD DAYS

UNIT TEST

Choose *two* of the following questions to answer in paragraph form. Use as much detail as possible to completely answer the question. Use extra paper in back of the book if needed.

1) Why did the Alaska Engineering Commission choose Ship Creek as the Alaska Railroad headquarters? How did this choice impact the city?

2) Describe the early days of Anchorage. How did the city get its name? What were the living conditions like? What caused the railroad workforce in Anchorage to be cut by almost half in 1918?

3) When was the Alaska railroad completed? What was done to commemorate the occasion? What mystery surrounded this ceremony?

_____
_____
_____
_____
_____
_____
_____
_____
_____
_____
_____
_____
_____
_____
_____
_____
_____
_____
_____
_____
_____

UNIT 2: EARLY RAILROAD DAYS

Review Questions _____ (possible 9 pts.)
Fill-the-Blanks _____ (possible 11 pts.)

Unit Test
Essay 1
Demonstrates understanding of the topic _____ (possible 5 pts.)
Answered the questions completely and accurately _____ (possible 5 pts.)
Composition is neat _____ (possible 5 pts.)
Grammar and Spelling _____ (possible 5 pts.)

Essay 2
Demonstrates understanding of the topic _____ (possible 5 pts.)
Answered the questions completely and accurately _____ (possible 5 pts.)
Composition is neat _____ (possible 5 pts.)
Grammar and Spelling _____ (possible 5 pts.)

Subtotal Points _____ **(possible 60 pts.)**

Extra Credit
Word Puzzle _____ (5 pt. per completed puzzle)
Complete an Enrichment Activity _____ (possible 5 pts.)
Oral presentation _____ (possible 10 pts.)

Total Extra Credit _____

Total Unit Points _____

GRADE CHART

A   54-60+ points

B   48-53 points

C   42-47 points

D   36-41 points

UNIT 3: BIG CITY CONCERNS

LESSON 7: VOTERS CHOOSE SELF-RULE
LESSON 8: FIRST MAYOR TACKLES VICE

Note: Read both chapters 7 and 8 before completing this lesson.

FACTS TO KNOW

Petition – A formal written request typically signed by many people

Judge Frederick Brown – Judge of the Third Judicial Division in Valdez who granted Anchorage residents their first local election

Mayor Leopold David – The first mayor of Anchorage

Prohibition – A ban on production, transportation and sale of alcoholic beverages

COMPREHENSION QUESTIONS

1) Why did a group of Anchorage citizens file a petition with the U.S. District Court at Valdez in 1920? What did the petition say? _____

_____

_____

_____

2) What were the results of the election ordered by Judge Frederick Brown? What ruling did Judge Brown make after the election? _____

_____

_____

_____

3) What was Mayor Leopold David's primary responsibility when he was elected in 1920? What laws did he put into place? _____

_____

_____

_____

4) What were some of the issues that Mayor David faced as the new mayor? Why was bootlegging a problem in Alaska in the early 1900s? _____

_____

_____

_____

DISCUSSION QUESTION

(Discuss this question with your teacher or write your answer in essay form below. Use additional paper if necessary.)

Why do you think the people of Anchorage wanted to elect their leaders? How was this different than having the Alaska Railroad Commission govern their day to day affairs?

_____
_____
_____
_____
_____
_____
_____
_____
_____
_____
_____
_____
_____
_____
_____
_____
_____
_____

ENRICHMENT ACTIVITY

Write a letter to a local politician. You can write about a problem that you see in your community, something you would like to see in your neighborhood or simply a letter of encouragement.

Use this Website link for more ideas and information on how to find the right person to send your letter to: https://www.education.com/magazine/article/How_Write_Letter_Politician/

LEARN MORE

Read more about early Anchorage history by visiting http://www.cookinlethistory.org/anchorage-history.html

UNIT 3: BIG CITY CONCERNS

LESSON 10: FIRST POLICE CHIEF MURDERED

FACTS TO KNOW

Anchorage City Council – Elected city government leaders in Anchorage
John "Jack" Sturgus – The first chief of police in Anchorage
Vice – Immoral and criminal activities

COMPREHENSION QUESTIONS

1) According to author Kenneth Gideon, how did bootleggers work around Anchorage's prohibition laws in the early 1900s? _____
_____
_____
_____

2) What important issue did the Anchorage City Council ask Chief Sturgus to focus on?
_____
_____
_____
_____

3) What happened to John Sturgus within a few weeks of working as police chief?
_____
_____
_____
_____

4) Describe some of the theories people had about what happened to John Sturgus. ____
_____
_____
_____
_____

DISCUSSION QUESTION

(Discuss this question with your teacher or write your answer in essay form below. Use additional paper if necessary.)

How would you approach the vice problems that Anchorage had when John Sturgus was hired? Would you do things differently? Explain how you would have handled the problems.

_____

_____
_____
_____
_____
_____
_____
_____
_____
_____
_____
_____
_____
_____
_____
_____
_____
_____

ENRICHMENT ACTIVITY

Law enforcement has the very difficult job of protecting and serving our communities. Take some time to get to know more about your local police department by either visiting its Website or visit your local police station in person. If you decide to visit in person, prepare two or three questions to bring with you.

LEARN MORE

Read more about the history of police in the United States and other parts of the world by visiting https://www.britannica.com/topic/police

UNIT 4: A FEW CITY FOREFATHERS
LESSON 9: PIONEER PHILANTHROPIST ARRIVES

FACTS TO KNOW

Zachariah J. Loussac – One of Anchorage's first philanthropists
Philanthropist – A person who seeks to help others, often by being generous with money

COMPREHENSION QUESTIONS

1) What led Z.J. Loussac to travel from New York to Alaska? _____
_____
_____
_____
_____

2) What happened the first two times that Loussac attempted to make it to Alaska?
_____
_____
_____
_____
_____

3) How did he advertise his drugstore in Anchorage? What did he offer in his drugstore?
_____
_____
_____
_____
_____

4) How did Loussac describe the amount of money that he made during World War II?
_____
_____
_____
_____

5) What gift was hailed as the "most generous gesture ever made by a living Alaskan toward his fellow Alaskans"?

_____

_____

_____

_____

6) What did Loussac say was the best thing that happened to him in Anchorage?

_____

_____

_____

_____

DISCUSSION QUESTION

(Discuss this question with your teacher or write your answer in essay form below. Use additional paper if necessary.)

Do you think that Zachariah Loussac had more fun making a lot of money or giving a lot of money away? Explain your answer.

_____

_____

_____

_____

_____

_____

_____

_____

_____

_____

_____

_____

_____

ENRICHMENT ACTIVITY

Imagine that you were given $1 million that you can use to help others. How would you spend it? Write a paragraph or two about what you would do with the money.

LEARN MORE

Read more about Z.J. Loussac by visiting http://www.jmaw.org/loussac-jewish-mayor-anchorage-alaska/

UNIT 4: A FEW CITY FOREFATHERS

LESSON 11: "CAP" LATHROP GAMBLES ON ALASKA

FACTS TO KNOW

Austin E. "Cap" Lathrop – One of Alaska's greatest entrepreneurs who became involved in transportation, entertainment, coal and radio, among other things, in Alaska

L.J. Perry – Austin E. "Cap" Lathrop's steamboat

"The Cheechakos" – The first full-length motion picture filmed entirely in Alaska

COMPREHENSION QUESTIONS

1) Why did the discovery of gold in the Turnagain Arm area of Cook Inlet interest Cap Lathrop? _____

_____

_____

2) Describe the work of a steamboat crew. _____

_____

_____

_____

3) Why were movies important in the Last Frontier? _____

_____

_____

_____

4) What was the only movie made by the Alaska Motion Picture Corporation? What was it about? _____

_____

_____

_____

5) After his movie failed, in what other businesses did Austin Lathrop get involved?

_____

_____

_____

_____

DISCUSSION QUESTION

(Discuss this question with your teacher or write your answer in essay form below. Use additional paper if necessary.)

One of the reasons that Austin Lathrop's movie failed in New York was because of the title, *The Cheechakos*. Reread the description of the movie on Pages 106-107. What would you name the movie? Why?

_____

_____

_____

_____

_____

_____

_____

_____

_____

_____

_____

_____

_____

_____

_____

_____

_____

_____

ENRICHMENT ACTIVITY

Watch this short video about the making of Alaska's first full-length motion picture by visiting https://vimeo.com/117362265

LEARN MORE

Read more about steamboat transportation by visiting http://www.akhistorycourse.org/americas-territory/rivers-get-people-and-freight-inland

UNIT 4: A FEW CITY FOREFATHERS
LESSON 12: "MR. BASEBALL" HITS TOWN

FACTS TO KNOW

William F. Mulcahy – Alaska's first National Baseball Congress Commissioner, also known as "Mr. Baseball"

Gertrude Mulcahy – Mr. Baseball's (William Mulcahy) wife

COMPREHENSION QUESTIONS

1) What position led William Mulcahy to move from Connecticut to Anchorage? What common interest did he find with the other railroad workers? _____

_____

_____

_____

2) How did he become involved with the baseball league in 1923? _____

_____

_____

_____

_____

3) According to his wife, Gertrude, the railroad company employment manager would ask applicants what position they played in baseball. Why did he ask this question?

_____

_____

_____

_____

4) What was Gertrude's nickname? Why? _____

_____

_____

_____

5) Why did William Mulcahy promote youth sports? _____

_____

_____

_____

6) How did the city of Anchorage honor Mr. Baseball in 1951 and again in 1964?

_____

_____

_____

DISCUSSION QUESTION

(Discuss this question with your teacher or write your answer in essay form below. Use additional paper if necessary.)

Why do you think baseball was such a popular sport for railroad workers?

_____

_____

_____

_____

_____

_____

_____

_____

_____

_____

_____

_____

_____

_____

_____

_____

_____

LEARN MORE

Read about the history of the Alaska Baseball League by visiting http://www.alaskabaseballleague.org/view/alaskabaseballleague/history-127/alaska-baseball-history-2

TIME TO REVIEW

Review Chapters 7-12 of your book before moving on the Unit Review. See how many questions you can answer without looking at your book.

UNIT 3: BIG CITY CONCERNS
UNIT 4: A FEW FOREFATHERS

REVIEW LESSONS 7-12

Write down what you remember about:

Petition _____

_____

Judge Frederick Brown _____

_____

Mayor Leopold David _____

_____

Prohibition _____

_____

Anchorage City Council _____

_____

John "Jack" Sturgus _____

_____

Vice _____

_____

Zachariah J. Loussac _____

_____

Philanthropist _____

_____

Austin E. "Cap" Lathrop _____

_____

L.J. Perry _____

_____

William F. Mulcahy _____

_____

Gertrude Mulcahy _____

_____

Fill in the blanks:

1) Technically speaking, Anchorage was born in November _____, when a group of Anchorage citizens filed a _____ for a special election be held to determine whether the majority of residents wanted the _____ to continue to govern the day to day affairs, or if _____ should take over management of the town.

2) The election returns showed a count of _____ votes for incorporation and _____ votes against. Another 85 _____ ballots had been stuffed into the ballot box. After careful consideration, _____ ruled the 85 _____ votes were to be ignored. Anchorage became a city on Nov. 23, _____.

3) When Judge _____ became Anchorage's first _____, he helped the new city _____ develop ordinances to provide law and order.

4) Mayor _____ and the city council tried to curtail _____ by adopting a "_____," which required an unobstructed view from the street into "pool halls, cigar stores, soft-drink emporiums, and other businesses of a similar character."

5) Since _____ provided a revenue stream for so many of Anchorage's citizens, Mayor _____, who died of heart disease in 1924 at 43, found it virtually impossible to keep _____ from flowing in the frontier town.

6) So in an effort to control the _____ in Anchorage, Mayor _____ and the _____ authorized the establishment of the city's first _____ soon after the city became incorporated. But tragedy soon hit that new department. The first _____ was murdered shortly after taking his post.

7) The _____ offered several _____ for the murder of _____. One suggested the chief was killed _____ _____.

8) The _____ time proved to be the charm for _____, when he opened a _____ in Anchorage. The mushroom growth of Anchorage during _____ was the turning point for his business. Not only was he able to pay off all his debts, but he found money "rolling in by the _____!"

9) In 1946, _____ set up the _____,
which he dedicated to the recreational, cultural, scientific or educational activities in the
_____ area. He wanted to do something for _____ –
the city had been so good to him – and decided to give it _____.

10) _____ plied the waters of Cook Inlet carrying _____
_____ for several years. He also dabbled in _____
_____ until the federal government set aside millions of acres of public land
for reserves.

11) In 1922, several Anchorage residents decided to go into the _____
business themselves. They formed the _____ and
elected _____, who owned theaters in Anchorage, Fairbanks, Seward,
Valdez and Cordova, as president. The businessmen raised $75,000 (more than $1 million
in 2017 dollars) to produce a 12-reel picture titled _____.

12) In September 1922,_____ hired on from the New York, New
Heaven and Hartford Railway to take the position of _____ for the
_____.

13) In 1923, _____ became president of the _____, as
well as its treasurer, secretary, groundskeeper and ticket seller.

14) Besides his work with adult baseball, _____ became deeply
involved in recreation for the _____ of Anchorage. He believed sports
to be an answer to the problem of _____.

Early Alaska Movers & Shakers
Word Scramble Puzzle
Unscramble the words below

1. wraned eicshrnsent		Land Office chief for Alaska Engineering Commission
2. crrifdkee nworb		Judge who ordered a special election in Anchorage in 1920
3. polldoe dviad		First elected Anchorage mayor
4. kafrn erde		As a child, he sold bottles to bootleggers
5. ajkc utssrgu		First chief of police
6. csora eorsnadn		First butcher
7. hrzcaaia lucsaso		Anchorage's first philanthropist
8. ebn eoebk		City clerk when ZJ Loussac was mayor
9. **iutans oartlph**		One of Alaska's greatest industrialists
10. ilwlima ymluhac		Known as Mr. Baseball

UNIT 3: BIG CITY CONCERNS
UNIT 4: A FEW FOREFATHERS

UNIT TEST

Choose *three* of the following questions to answer in paragraph form. Use as much detail as possible to completely answer the question. Use extra paper in back of the book if needed.

1) Describe how Anchorage residents took over management of their town. What did they do to request an election? What were the results of the election?

2) What were some of the challenges that law enforcement faced in early Anchorage? How did they approach these problems?

3) What happened to the first police chief of Anchorage? Describe some of the theories about this mystery.

4) Summarize the journey of Zachariah Loussac from a poor kid in Russia to a wealthy philanthropist in Alaska. Why is he known as Alaska's first philanthropist?

5) Describe at least two of "Cap" Lanthrop's business ventures. Were these ventures successful? Why or why not?

6) Who was Mr. Baseball? How did he get involved in the baseball league in Alaska? Why did he promote youth sports?

_____
_____
_____
_____
_____
_____
_____
_____
_____
_____
_____
_____

UNIT 3: BIG CITY CONCERNS
UNIT 4: A FEW FOREFATHERS

Review Questions _____ (possible 13 pts.)
Fill-the-Blanks _____ (possible 14 pts.)

Unit Test

Essay 1
Demonstrates understanding of the topic _____ (possible 5 pts.)
Answered the questions completely and accurately _____ (possible 5 pts.)
Composition is neat _____ (possible 5 pts.)
Grammar and Spelling _____ (possible 5 pts.)

Essay 2
Demonstrates understanding of the topic _____ (possible 5 pts.)
Answered the questions completely and accurately _____ (possible 5 pts.)
Composition is neat _____ (possible 5 pts.)
Grammar and Spelling _____ (possible 5 pts.)

Essay 3
Demonstrates understanding of the topic _____ (possible 5 pts.)
Answered the questions completely and accurately _____ (possible 5 pts.)
Composition is neat _____ (possible 5 pts.)
Grammar and Spelling _____ (possible 5 pts.)

Subtotal Points _____ **(possible 87 pts.)**

Extra Credit
Word Puzzle _____ (5 pt. per completed puzzle)
Complete an Enrichment Activity _____ (possible 5 pts.)
Oral presentation _____ (possible 10 pts.)

Total Extra Credit _____

Total Unit Points _____

GRADE CHART

A 79-87+ points

B 70-78 points

C 61-69 points

D 52-60 points

Baseball became a popular sport all across Alaska, as seen in this photograph of John Oktollik in the Pribilof Islands in the 1900s.

UNIT 5: TRAILBLAZERS ON WHEELS

LESSON 13: A VERY BUMPY RIDE

FACTS TO KNOW

Robert E. "Bobby" Sheldon – He built the first car in Alaska
Invention – The creation of a device or process after study and experimentation

COMPREHENSION QUESTIONS

1) How much experience did Robert Sheldon have with automobiles before building the first car in Alaska? How did he learn how to build a car? _____

_____

_____

_____

_____

2) What was Robert Sheldon's first job at age 14? What first did he accomplish in this job?

_____

_____

_____

_____

_____

3) What inspired Robert Sheldon to build a car? _____

_____

_____

_____

_____

4) Why did he quit his job at Northern Commercial Power Plant? What "impossible" task did he set out to do in 1913? _____

_____

_____

_____

_____

5) What business did Sheldon start after becoming the first man to ride a bike from Valdez to Fairbanks? _____

_____

_____

_____

6) When he left the transportation business in 1926, what did he do for work?

_____

_____

_____

_____

DISCUSSION QUESTION

(Discuss this question with your teacher or write your answer in essay form below. Use additional paper if necessary.)

Robert Sheldon often said, "Who wants to be the richest man in the cemetery?" What do you think he meant by this question?

_____

_____

_____

_____

_____

_____

_____

_____

_____

_____

_____

_____

ENRICHMENT ACTIVITY

Read more about Model-T cars and how they changed America by visiting
http://www.history.com/topics/automobiles

LEARN MORE

Look for this article at your local library:
"But We Kept 'em Going," in THE ALASKA JOURNAL 11 (1981): 237-240.
Monaghan, Patricia and Roland Wulbert

UNIT 5: TRAILBLAZERS ON WHEELS

LESSON 14: A REO AND A RESORT
LESSON 15: ALASKA'S FIRST STREETCAR

Note: Read both chapters 14 and 15 before completing this lesson.

FACTS TO KNOW

Joe Spenard – He drove the first auto truck in Anchorage and ran a taxi service
Lake Spenard – Anchorage lakeside resort that Joe Spenard opened in 1916
Martin Itjen – Built, owned and operated a streetcar in Skagway

COMPREHENSION QUESTIONS

1) What did Joe Spenard do after moving from Valdez to Anchorage? _____
_____
_____
_____
_____

2) Why was the area known as "Miracle Mile" important to the growth of Anchorage?
_____
_____
_____
_____
_____

3) What discovery did Joe Spenard make as he was clearing trees? What did he do after he made this discovery? _____
_____
_____
_____
_____

4) Why did he sell the resort in 1917? What happened to Lake Spenard after Joe left?
_____
_____
_____
_____

5) What led Martin Itjen to start Skagway Streetcar Company? _____

_____

_____

_____

6) How did Martin Itjen entertain his customers? What were his streetcars like?

_____

_____

_____

_____

7) Why did Martin Itjen travel to Hollywood, California? _____

_____

_____

_____

DISCUSSION QUESTION

(Discuss this question with your teacher or write your answer in essay form below. Use additional paper if necessary.)

What type of transportation did Alaskans rely on before motorized vehicles? Name some of the ways that motorized vehicles changed their way of life?

_____

_____

_____

_____

_____

ENRICHMENT ACTIVITY

Have you ever wondered who invented an everyday item like your bicycle, eyeglasses, pencil or refrigerator? Spend some time at your local library to research three common, everyday items and the people that invented them. Take notes on what you learn. Present what you learn to the class.

LEARN MORE

Read more about early automobiles in Alaska by visiting
http://www.akhistorycourse.org/americas-territory/overland-routes-develop

Early Transportation in Alaska
Word Search Puzzle
Find the words listed below

```
X Q Y Y Z L V E L C Y C I B S V A G L E
K V H I Q L Q E S R O H S L E D B K B C
J I E M T C J D B D N S V S A J S D U L
I X L A L R U F Y I R E M A E T S G L H
J A O R D U A Z H T S L E E H W C I O V
E T P T R R F N O T A Y K V N O S H E S
P N R I R F A M S G C S R T O M B T G X
T W G N B P S N I P D H T P D U O P A P
J B W I O C L S E A O A D R L U O D I N
C S X T N W B X O P L R K E E K P V R V
B G C J U E X R F Q S E T K H E L Z R R
X A W E Q Z L M I L L E B A S J T B A F
C V A N R I B E T I C W O L T S M C C F
I W G Y A A K O B T E H G J R I G G A O
N L O R A Z J O L N G T H A E I O O A R
A P N N E F M E F M Q R H N B M R N D X
H P S S F O D F E X O U Q B O U A R M U
C Z C J T O Z T I C V C C R R D G O J O
E C Q U M F S Q Q W G K B P R W S G L C
M R A U C V N S A F I K A Q U Q S I Y A
```

ROBERT SHELDON	JOE SPENARD	MARTIN ITJEN
BUGGY	WHEELS	ENGINE
WAGONS	SLED	DOGS
MECHANIC	STEAMER	RAILROAD
TRANSPORTATION	AUTOMOBILE	MODEL T
HORSE	BICYCLE	TRUCK
TAXI	STREETCAR	CARRIAGE

While automobiles brought a new way to travel around Alaska, as seen in the photograph above of a loaded Model T touring car in front of a roadhouse, the lack of proper roads caused some problems, as seen in the photo below of a Model T stuck in mud.

UNIT 6: EPIDEMICS, RESCUES AND DISASTER

LESSON 16: THE BIG SICKNESS

FACTS TO KNOW

Influenza – Contagious viral infection that often occurs in epidemics
Epidemic – Widespread occurrence of a disease in a community at the same time
Thomas Riggs – Governor of Alaska Territory from 1918 to 1921

COMPREHENSION QUESTIONS

1) Called the _____, only because the _____
press wrote about it, the virus took more than _____ American lives
between 1918-1919. Fatality estimates worldwide range from _____ million to
_____ million.

2) How did Alaska Territorial Gov. Thomas Riggs attempt to keep influenza away from
Alaska's residents? _____
_____
_____
_____

3) What caused influenza to rapidly spread in the Seward Peninsula? _____
_____
_____
_____

4) What previous events caused the Native people of Alaska to fear sickness brought by
non-Natives? Describe some of the Alaska Natives' beliefs about sickness. _____
_____
_____
_____
_____

5) How did Gov. Thomas Riggs describe the flu epidemic in Alaska? _____
_____
_____
_____
_____

DISCUSSION QUESTION

(Discuss this question with your teacher or write your answer in essay form below. Use additional paper if necessary.)

Why do you think influenza does not kill as many people today as it did between 1918-1919?

_____
_____
_____
_____
_____
_____
_____
_____
_____
_____
_____
_____
_____
_____
_____

ENRICHMENT ACTIVITY

Imagine that you are a doctor in 1918 during the influenza epidemic. Create a poster to educate the public about ways that they can prevent the flu. Consider what you know about how to protect yourself from catching the flu. Keep in mind that the first flu vaccines were not developed until the 1930s.

LEARN MORE

Read more about the influenza epidemic and other diseases that affected early Alaska history by visiting http://www.akhistorycourse.org/americas-territory/alaskas-heritage/chapter-4-21-health-and-medicine

UNIT 6: EPIDEMICS, RESCUES AND DISASTER

LESSON 17: DISASTER STRIKES SOUTHEAST

FACTS TO KNOW

Princess Sophia – Canadian steamer that sunk in 1918 killing more than 350 people

Captain Leonard Locke – Captain of the *Princess Sophia*

Vanderbilt Reef – Rocky area just visible above the water's surface in Southeast Alaska's Lynn Canal

COMPREHENSION QUESTIONS

1) Who was traveling on the *Princess Sophia* when it pulled out of the port at Skagway in October 1918? _____

_____

_____

_____

2) Describe the *Princess Sophia*. Was it considered a safe ship? _____

_____

_____

_____

_____

3) What was the weather like a few hours after the steamer left Skagway? How did the ship get off course? _____

_____

_____

_____

_____

4) What happened when the *Princess Sophia* reached Vanderbilt Reef at 2 a.m?

_____

_____

_____

_____

5) How did the *Princess Sophia* sink? Did anyone survive? _____

_____

_____

_____

_____

DISCUSSION QUESTION

(Discuss this question with your teacher or write your answer in essay form below. Use additional paper if necessary.)

Why was the sinking of *Princess Sophia* devastating to Dawson City?

_____

_____

_____

_____

_____

_____

_____

_____

_____

_____

_____

_____

_____

_____

_____

_____

_____

ENRICHMENT ACTIVITY

Watch this short YouTube video to learn more about the *Princess Sophia* tragedy: https://www.youtube.com/watch?v=S3DSMyZb5dc

LEARN MORE

Look for this book at your local library:
SOS North Pacific, Gordon R. Newell. Portland, Oregon: Binford and Mort, 1955.

UNIT 6: EPIDEMICS, RESCUES AND DISASTER

LESSON 18: FIRST RELAY RUN NORTH

FACTS TO KNOW

Dr. John B. Beeson – Alaska railroad doctor who traveled 500 miles on the Iditarod Trail to help Claude Baker

Claude Baker – Iditarod banker who was near death from an injury in 1921

COMPREHENSION QUESTIONS

1) Why did Dr. John Beeson travel to Iditarod in 1921? _____
_____
_____
_____

2) How did he travel there? _____
_____
_____
_____

3) How long did it take him to get to Iditarod? Who helped the dog team relay to run smoothly? _____
_____
_____
_____

4) How was the return trip different? _____
_____
_____
_____

DISCUSSION QUESTION

(Discuss this question with your teacher or write your answer in essay form below. Use additional paper if necessary.)

What do you think the definition of a hero is? Would you call Dr. Beeson a hero? Why or why not?

LEARN MORE

Learn more about ways that Alaska Natives promoted health, reduced pain and met the challenges of life by visiting http://www.akhistorycourse.org/alaskas-cultures/alaska-natives-and-health

MAP ACTIVITY

Using the map below, trace Dr. Beeson's route after he got off the railroad train in Nenana. Find the following places he raced through on his way to save the banker's life in Iditarod: 1) Manley Hot Springs   2) Tanana   3) Ruby   4) Poorman   5) Cripple 6) Ophir   7) Iditarod

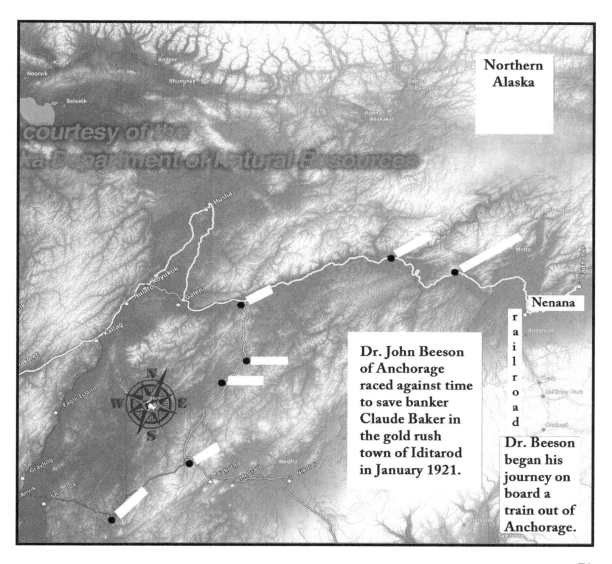

Northern Alaska

Nenana

r a i l r o a d

Dr. John Beeson of Anchorage raced against time to save banker Claude Baker in the gold rush town of Iditarod in January 1921.

Dr. Beeson began his journey on board a train out of Anchorage.

UNIT 6: EPIDEMICS, RESCUES AND DISASTER

LESSON 19: DIPHTHERIA THREATENS NOME

FACTS TO KNOW

Diphtheria – Highly contagious disease that killed several people in Nome in the 1920s

Dr. Curtis Welch – Physician in Nome who sent for antitoxin to stop the diphtheria outbreak there

Leonhard Seppala – Legendary musher who helped carry the diphtheria serum to Nome

COMPREHENSION QUESTIONS

1) What did Dr. Curtis Welch do when he saw the grayish patches of diphtheria membranes in 7-year-old Bessie Stanley on Jan. 2, 1925? _____

_____

_____

_____

2) How is diphtheria spread from person to person? What is the cure?

_____

_____

_____

_____

3) Why did Dr. Welch expect that there would be a large number of deaths in Alaska Native population of Nome without the antitoxin? _____

_____

_____

_____

4) Who was able to send the first shipment of antitoxin to Nome in 1921? How long did it take to get there? _____

_____

_____

_____

5) Who were Balto and Togo? Why were they considered the real heroes of the relay teams that brought the antitoxin to Nome? How were they honored after the serum was delivered to Nome? _____

_____

_____

_____

DISCUSSION QUESTION

(Discuss this question with your teacher or write your answer in essay form below. Use additional paper if necessary.)

What did you learn about dogs in this lesson? Why do you think they were the best kind of animal to pull sleds as means of long-distance transportation in Alaska?

_____

_____

_____

_____

_____

_____

_____

_____

_____

_____

_____

_____

_____

_____

_____

LEARN MORE

Look for this book at your local library:
Everything I Know About Training and Racing Sled Dogs, George Attla. Rome, New York: Arner Publications, 1974

TIME TO REVIEW

Review Chapters 13-19 of your book before moving on the Unit Review. See how many questions you can answer without looking at your book.

Epidemics, Rescues and Disasters
Crossword Puzzle

Read Across and Down clues and fill in blank boxes that match numbers on the clues

Across

3 Infectious disease that spreads widely and affects many people at the same time
5 Alaska village where scientists unearthed victims of the 1918 flu in the late 1990s to study their DNA
8 Musher that took serum from Nenana to Minto and was first musher in the relay toward Nome
10 Captain of the steamship that hit reef in Southeast Alaska in 1918
12 Alaska governor who tried to keep flu away from the north
15 Alaska governor when 1925 serum run to Nome happened
18 Nurse who helped doctor in Nome diagnose sick people in 1925
20 Method by which doctor traveled to Iditarod to save banker's life
22 Name of reef that the steamship hit in October 1918
24 First man to summit Denali who was on board the ship that sank in Southeast Alaska in 1918
25 A strict isolation imposed to prevent the spread of disease
27 Famous serum-run dog is stuffed and on display at the Iditarod Museum in this Alaska town
28 Banker who was desperately ill in Iditarod in January 1921
29 Doctor's first time mushing was because this fellow misjudged a turn and crashed on the way to Iditarod to save a banker's life
32 Doctor who raced from Anchorage to Iditarod to save a banker's life
34 Condition when wind and blowing snow made it difficult for dogs and mushers to see the trail on the way to Nome in 1925
35 A group of people or animals engaged in a task or activity for a fixed period of time and then replaced by a similar group
37 Lead dog that pulled into Nome with life-saving serum on Feb. 2, 1925
38 Place where Leonhard Seppala is buried
39 First reported case of flu in Alaska was in this town

Down

1 Sole survivor of the ship that sunk in Southeast Alaska in October 1918
2 These people were suspected of carrying the flu to several Alaska villages
4 Steamship that sank in Southeast Alaska in October 1918
6 Ship that carried flu to Nome in October 1918
7 Flu never made it to this northern Alaska village because of strict quarantine
9 Famous musher who helped doctor get back to Anchorage after saving the banker in Iditarod
11 Flu that killed millions during 1918-1919
13 About $1 million of this ore was on board the steamship that sank in Southeast Alaska in 1918
14 Type of sled dog
16 People feared that this would spread like wildlife in Nome in 1925

Epidemics, Rescues and Disasters
Crossword Puzzle

Down (Continued)

17 Leonhard Seppala's lead dog that traveled two to three times farther than any other dog team in the serum relay to Nome

19 Musher who pulled onto Front Street in Nome with the serum to save lives in February 1925

21 Alaska Railroad conductor who carried the serum from Anchorage to Nenana in 1925

23 Village where Dr. Curtis Welch saw symptoms of tonsillitis in 2-year old Inuit girl who then died in January 1925

26 Alaska village that paired men and women for marriage so orphans of the flu epidemic would have homes

30 River on which the doctor traveled to get to Iditarod in 1921

31 This is made from the serum of immunized horses and helps stop disease

33 Medicine that is injected into someone's blood to protect them against a poison or disease

36 Everyone in this Alaska village died from the flu of 1918

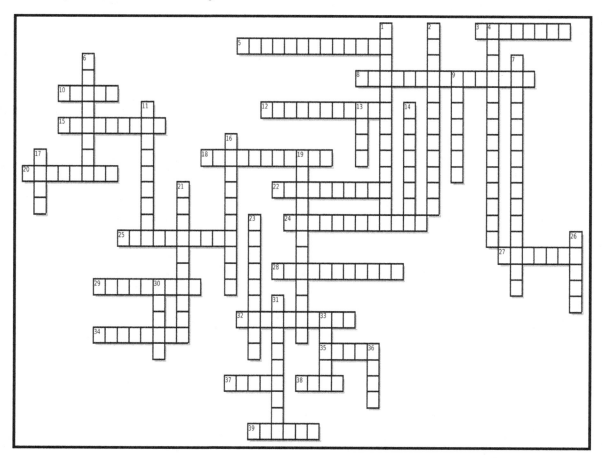

UNIT 5: TRAILBLAZERS ON WHEELS
UNIT 6: EPIDEMICS, RESCUES AND DISASTER

REVIEW LESSONS 13-19

Write down what you remember about:

Bobby E. "Bobby" Sheldon _____

_____

Invention _____

_____

Joe Spenard _____

_____

Lake Spenard _____

_____

Martin Itjen _____

_____

Influenza _____

_____

Epidemic _____

_____

Thomas Riggs _____

_____

Princess Sophia _____

_____

Captain Leonard Locke _____

_____

Vanderbilt Reef _____

_____

Dr. John B. Beeson _____

_____

Claude Baker _____

_____

Diphtheria _____

_____

Dr. Curtis Welch _____

_____

Leonhard Seppala _____

_____

Fill in the blanks:

1) On July 29, 1913, one of Alaska's trailblazers started on a historic journey – the first _____ trip over the wagon trail from _____ to _____. But that wasn't _____ first experience with a _____. _____, who'd never seen an _____, also built the first _____ in Alaska.

2) Shortly after arriving in _____, _____ sold the Model-T for $1,300 and bought a _____. He then pedaled back to _____ to become the first person to ride a _____ from _____ to the interior city. When he returned to _____, _____ ordered more Model-Ts and organized _____.

3) _____ moved to Anchorage from Valdez, where he'd had a small transfer business. Once he got settled in the new town, he purchased his _____ – said to be the first _____ in Anchorage.

4) While wandering through the timbered land one day, _____ found a _____ a few miles from the railroad community. There he set up a camp. He also made improvements to the land, which included a _____ with a roadhouse, bathhouses and a swimming beach. The area become known as

_____.

5) _____, an immigrant who came north from Florida in 1898 to join the stampede in search of riches in the _____ took _____ _____ on an excursion in a painted coal truck. After seeing how much _____ enjoyed the tour, he figured he could make a living off tourism in the famous gold rush city and started the _____.

6) In Alaska's only _____, 65-year-old sourdough _____, who was _____'s undertaker in the roaring days of the gold rush, traveled to the Continental United States to see _____, the movie actress.

7) During the spring of 1918, a _____ had spread across the world and sickened many people – and many died. Called the _____, only because the Spanish press wrote about it, the virus took more than _____ American lives between _____. Deaths worldwide range from _____ million to _____ million.

8) Alaska Gov. _____, who recognized that the deeply rooted Native culture of _____ might be aiding in the spread of the disease, issued a directive on Nov. 7 to try and stem the tide of Native deaths. He advised them "to _____and repel all _____; to avoid _____ within their villages; indeed, to avoid all _____, even those most vital to their self-esteem.

9) The Canadian Pacific Railway steamship _____ pulled out of the port at _____ around 10 p.m. on Oct. 23, 1918, and headed into the _____ Canal bound for Vancouver. One of the last ships scheduled to leave that fall, the 245-foot ship was filled with _____ gold miners, families and others heading south for the winter.

10) About 40 hours after she settled on the _____, the sea picked up _____'s stern and turned her 180 degrees, slipping her off the _____ – tearing her bottom out as she went. The sinking of the _____ devastated _____ City, as many of its professionals and businesspeople were on board the ill-fated steamer. It also was reported that _____was in her hold.

11) Early on the morning of Jan. 24, 1921, _____ hopped on a train leaving _____ and headed toward _____ after getting word through the U.S. Army Signal Corps that _____ was near death.

12) _____ pulled into _____, by _____, five and a half days days after stepping off the train in _____.

13) When _____ saw the grayish patches of _____ membranes in 7-year-old Bessie Stanley on Jan. 21, 1925, he sounded the alarm that triggered a race against time to stop a massive outbreak. Along with instituting _____, _____ sent radio telegrams via the U.S. Army Signal Corps to all the major towns and officials in Alaska. He desperately needed _____.

14) The _____ that carried the life-saving _____ would follow the _____ from _____, which crossed the barren Alaska Interior, following the _____ River for 137 miles to the village of _____ at the junction with the Yukon River.

Gunnar Kaasen + Balto
in their Race to Nome.

UNIT 5: TRAILBLAZERS ON WHEELS
UNIT 6: EPIDEMICS, RESCUES AND DISASTER

Unit Test

Choose *three* of the following questions to answer in paragraph form. Use as much detail as possible to completely answer the question. Use extra paper in back of the book if needed.

1) What famous firsts did Robert Sheldon accomplish? Describe how he learned how to do these things.

2) What discovery did Joe Spenard make? How did he make this discovery? What did he do after he made this discovery?

3) What business did Martin Itjen start in Skagway? How did he come up with the idea? Why did he travel to Hollywood?

4) What epidemic took millions of lives around the world between 1918-1919? How did this epidemic affect Alaska? What did the governor do to try to stop the spread of this disease? How did it eventually stop?

5) Explain what happened to the *Princess Sophia* in October 1918. Why was this event devastating to Dawson City?

6) Why did Alaska Natives fear disease brought by Europeans? What did they believe about disease? What precautions were taken to stop the spread of disease among Native people?

7) Why were sled dogs considered heroes to many people in 1925? How were they honored around the United States?

_____

_____

_____

_____

_____

_____

UNIT 5: TRAILBLAZERS ON WHEELS
UNIT 6: EPIDEMICS, RESCUES AND DISASTER

Review Questions	_____	(possible 16 pts.)
Fill-the-Blanks	_____	(possible 14 pts.)

Unit Test

Essay 1

Demonstrates understanding of the topic	_____	(possible 5 pts.)
Answered the questions completely and accurately	_____	(possible 5 pts.)
Composition is neat	_____	(possible 5 pts.)
Grammar and Spelling	_____	(possible 5 pts.)

Essay 2

Demonstrates understanding of the topic	_____	(possible 5 pts.)
Answered the questions completely and accurately	_____	(possible 5 pts.)
Composition is neat	_____	(possible 5 pts.)
Grammar and Spelling	_____	(possible 5 pts.)

Essay 3

Demonstrates understanding of the topic	_____	(possible 5 pts.)
Answered the questions completely and accurately	_____	(possible 5 pts.)
Composition is neat	_____	(possible 5 pts.)
Grammar and Spelling	_____	(possible 5 pts.)

Subtotal Points _____ **(possible 90 pts.)**

Extra Credit

Word Puzzle	_____	(5 pt. per completed puzzle)
Complete an Enrichment Activity	_____	(possible 5 pts.)
Oral presentation	_____	(possible 10 pts.)

Total Extra Credit _____

Total Unit Points _____

GRADE CHART

A   81-90+ points

B   72-80 points

C   63-71 points

D   54-62 points

Courtesy Wikipedia

Lake Hood Seaplane Base started out as two smaller lakes: Lake Hood to the west and Lake Spenard, discovered by Joe Spenard in the early 1900s, to the east. The state began dredging out a canal in between the two to create seaplane takeoff and taxi lanes in the 1970s. Today, Lake Hood sees nearly 200 daily operations and has become the largest and busiest seaplane base in the world.

UNIT 7: EARLY ALASKA AVIATION

LESSON 20: MAGNIFICENT FLYING MACHINES

FACTS TO KNOW

Henry Peterson – Built Alaska's first airplane
Arthur Williams – Organized the first air show in Alaska with James Martin
James V. Martin – The first to fly in Alaska's skies
Black Wolf Squadron – Alaska flying expedition organized by Brig. Gen. William Mitchell

COMPREHENSION QUESTIONS

1) Who was the first man to venture into Alaska's skies on July 4, 1899?

_____

_____

_____

2) How did Henry Peterson build Alaska's first airplane? What was the plane like? What was the first flight like? _____

_____

_____

_____

3) Where did the first flight over Alaska take place? How did Arthur Williams get involved in it? _____

_____

_____

_____

4) Why did Brig. Gen William Mitchell organize the Black Wolf Squadron?

_____

_____

_____

_____

DISCUSSION QUESTION

(Discuss this question with your teacher or write your answer in essay form below. Use additional paper if necessary.)

What do you think are some of the benefits of air travel over other methods of transportation?

_____
_____
_____
_____
_____
_____
_____
_____
_____
_____
_____
_____
_____
_____
_____
_____
_____

ENRICHMENT ACTIVITY

Alaska's first flight was big news in 1920. Imagine that you are the journalist who got an exclusive interview with pilot James Martin. Write down 3-5 questions that you would ask him. Can you imagine how he might answer the questions?

LEARN MORE

Read more about early air transportation in Alaska by visiting http://www.akhistory-course.org/americas-territory/alaskas-heritage/chapter-4-12-air-transportation

UNIT 7: EARLY ALASKA AVIATION

LESSON 21: AVIATORS HEAD NORTH

FACTS TO KNOW

Aviator – A pilot, airman or airwoman
Charles Otis Hammontree – The first aviator to fly an amphibian aircraft in Anchorage
Roy Franklin Jones – Cook Inlet aviator who started a flying service in Ketchikan
Merle Sasseen – Well-known bush pilot

COMPREHENSION QUESTIONS

1) Describe Anchorage's first flight. Who flew the plane? What kind of plane was it? How did the aviator prepare for the flight?

2) Why did Roy Jones see a need for a flying service in Ketchikan? Why did he close the business after only a year and a half? _____

_____

_____

_____

3) How was the first landing strip in Anchorage made? Who was the first aviator to use it? _____

_____

_____

_____

4) What "mishaps" did Merle Sasseen have? _____

_____

_____

_____

5) How did Alaskan pilots typically dress to fly the early open-cockpit planes? _____

_____

_____

_____

DISCUSSION QUESTION

(Discuss this question with your teacher or write your answer in essay form below. Use additional paper if necessary.)

Why do think that towns like Fairbanks and Ketchikan held large celebrations when the first aircraft landed in their city?

_____
_____
_____
_____
_____
_____
_____
_____
_____
_____
_____
_____
_____
_____
_____

ENRICHMENT ACTIVITY

History is made up of numerous cause-and-effect relationships. No historical event happens in isolation. Part of historical study is learning how people, places, movements and events are interrelated. Consider what you have learned thus far about the history of Alaska. Write five cause-and-effect relationships that you notice from your reading. Example: After the Wright Brothers made the first flight in 1903, flying events began popping up across the country.

LEARN MORE

TOP COVER FOR AMERICA: THE AIR FORCE IN ALASKA, by John Haile Cloe and Michael F. Monaghan 1920-1983. Missoula, Montana: Pictorial Histories Publishing Company, 1984.

UNIT 7: EARLY ALASKA AVIATION

LESSON 22: STRANGE SIGHT SOARS OVER TELLER

FACTS TO KNOW

Dirigible – A lighter-than-air craft that is powered and steerable
Norge – Dirigible from Norway that traveled to the North Pole in 1926
Roald Amundsen – Famous explorer who traveled from Norway to Alaska in the
Norge

COMPREHENSION QUESTIONS

1) The _____ *Norge* left _____ to travel across the
_____ on May 11, 1926.

2) How did the city of Nome prepare for the arrival of *Norge*? _____
_____
_____
_____

3) What happened when the aircraft got to Alaska? How did it end up off course?
_____
_____
_____
_____

4) What did the crewmembers do with the *Norge* when it reached Teller?
_____
_____
_____
_____

5) What did this expedition over the North Pole confirm? _____
_____
_____
_____

DISCUSSION QUESTION

(Discuss this question with your teacher or write your answer in essay form below. Use additional paper if necessary.)

The introduction of air travel was big news in Alaska and all over the world. What new invention or technology is making big news today?

_____
_____
_____
_____
_____
_____
_____
_____
_____
_____
_____
_____
_____
_____
_____
_____
_____

LEARN MORE

Read more about the history of flight by visiting https://www.grc.nasa.gov/WWW/K-12/ UEET/StudentSite/historyofflight.html

MAP ACTIVITY

Locate the following places that you have been reading about in this unit on the map below: 1) Fairbanks   2) Anchorage   3) Ketchikan   4) Nome   5) Teller

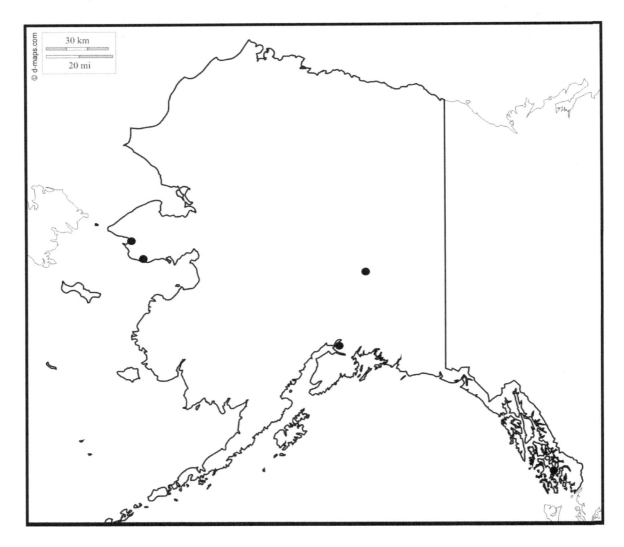

UNIT 7: EARLY ALASKA AVIATION

LESSON 23: CORDOVA FINALLY ENTERS AIR AGE

FACTS TO KNOW

Gorst Air Transport – Made plans to make the first trip across the Gulf of Alaska to Cordova

Gulf of Alaska – A broad inlet of the North Pacific on the south coast of Alaska

Clayton Scott – The first pilot to travel by airplane over the Gulf of Alaska to Cordova

COMPREHENSION QUESTIONS

1) When did aviation become important to Alaska? _____
_____
_____
_____

2) Why did it take so long for airplanes to come to Cordova? _____
_____
_____
_____

3) How did the city of Cordova plan to celebrate the arrival of the Gorst Air Transport Company aircraft? _____
_____
_____
_____

4) Explain why this historic event in Cordova didn't happen as scheduled.
_____
_____
_____
_____

5) What did pilot Clayon Scott say about Cordova and its residents after making the first aerial trip to the city? _____
_____
_____

DISCUSSION QUESTION

(Discuss this question with your teacher or write your answer in essay form below. Use additional paper if necessary.)

Why do you think the residents of Cordova were so eager to have aircraft come to their city?

_____
_____
_____
_____
_____
_____
_____
_____
_____
_____
_____
_____
_____
_____
_____
_____

LEARN MORE

Look for this book at your local library:
Alaska Aviation History, by Robert Stevens, 1990. Polynyas press, Des Moines, WA.

TIME TO REVIEW

Review Chapters 20-23 of your book before moving on the Unit Review. See how many questions you can answer without looking at your book.

Biplanes of the early 1900s took on many shapes, as seen in this photograph of Charles H. McNeil apparently sitting in one over Seattle.

UNIT 7: EARLY ALASKA AVIATION

REVIEW LESSONS 20-23

Write down what you remember about:

Henry Peterson _____

_____

Arthur Williams _____

_____

James V. Martin _____

_____

Black Wolf Squadron _____

_____

Aviator _____

_____

Charles Otis Hammontree _____

_____

Roy Franklin Jones _____

_____

Merle Sasseen _____

_____

Dirigible _____

_____

Norge _____

_____

Roald Amundsen _____

_____

Gorst Air Transport _____

_____

Gulf of Alaska _____

_____

Clayton Scott _____

_____

Fill in the blanks:

1) By 1911, flying events and air shows across the country were making news. And that's when _____ resident _____ decided to build Alaska's first _____. The would-be pilot, who had no flying experience but had read much about _____ the plane, attempted lift off. But the machine _____.

2) _____ was the first to fly in Alaska's skies when promoter _____ brought him north. The promoters thought they'd make a hefty profit with a Fourth of July _____.

3) Even though _____ found it too difficult to continue operating his flying service in _____ in the early 1920s, it wouldn't be long before _____ became one of the main modes of transportation in Southeast Alaska.

4) In the summer of 1923, _____ resident _____ believed that his community needed to enter the air age. He organized and led the entire town in clearing a _____ just beyond civilization for the town's first _____.

5) A typical aviator's outfit included two pairs of heavy wool _____, one pair of _____ socks, _____ that reached over the knees, heavy underwear, a pair of breeches, a pair of heavy trousers, a shirt and sweater, and a skin _____. The whole outfit then was covered with a knee-length _____. Wool _____ covered with heavy fur mitts protected their hands.

6) Famous explorer _____, who twice before had attempted to reach the _____ in conventional aircraft, realized his dream in the 348-foot airship called _____ after he joined forces with a couple other men who were familiar with dirigibles.

7) _____ residents were none too pleased when they learned that the huge craft – which had left _____ to fly over the North Pole a few days earlier – had missed their beautiful town and landed in _____ instead.

8) The first flight in Alaska soared in the skies of _____ in July _____. The _____ Squadron touched down in Wrangell, flew over Juneau and made its way to _____ in 1920. Then a seaplane made its debut in the waters of _____ near Anchorage in June 1922, and another flying boat landed in _____ a few weeks later. Even _____ had seen a huge dirigible land on its shores in 1926. But by 1929, the city of _____ had yet to see its first aircraft landing.

9) _____ Company canceled its plans to land in _____ after bad weather kicked up winds in May 1929. But the residents were cheered the next day when they received a report that one pilot, _____, offered to fly to _____ if four passengers could be secured.

Early Alaska Aircraft
Word Scramble
Unscramble the words below

1. toh ria onallbo   Professor Leonard took one of these up into the air in Juneau in 1899

2. nlapomoen   A plane with one set of wings

3. aplbien   A plane with multiple sets of wings

4. De nHadlvial   The type of plane that came north with the Black Wolf Squadron

5. apsealne   Type of plane that can take off and land on water

6. hanpiambi   Another name for planes that can take off and land on water

7. itrssuC yifgnl oabt   Pilot Roy Franklin Jones touched down in Ketchikan in one of these in 1922

8. Hoiss nSrddtaa   This type of plane was the first to fly in Anchorage in 1924

9. iiledgrib   The Norge was one of these

10. rracatfi   Another name for planes

UNIT 7: EARLY ALASKA AVIATION

Unit Test

Choose *three* of the following questions to answer in paragraph form. Use as much detail as possible to completely answer the question. Use extra paper in back of the book if needed.

1) Describe the first flight over Alaska. Who flew the plane? Where did he fly? How did Alaskans react to this historical event?

2) What are some of the ways air transportation impacted Alaska's history? Why was it so important to many Alaskans?

3) How did Roald Amundsen and his crew disappoint the residents of Nome in 1926? Explain what happened.

4) Why did it take so long for aviators to travel to Cordova? Who finally made the trip there? What did he say about Cordova after making the trip?

UNIT 7: EARLY ALASKA AVIATION

Review Questions   _____ (possible 14 pts.)
Fill-the-Blanks   _____ (possible 9 pts.)

Unit Test
Essay 1
     Demonstrates understanding of the topic   _____ (possible 5 pts.)
     Answered the questions completely and accurately   _____ (possible 5 pts.)
     Composition is neat   _____ (possible 5 pts.)
     Grammar and Spelling   _____ (possible 5 pts.)

Essay 2
     Demonstrates understanding of the topic   _____ (possible 5 pts.)
     Answered the questions completely and accurately   _____ (possible 5 pts.)
     Composition is neat   _____ (possible 5 pts.)
     Grammar and Spelling   _____ (possible 5 pts.)

Essay 3
     Demonstrates understanding of the topic   _____ (possible 5 pts.)
     Answered the questions completely and accurately   _____ (possible 5 pts.)
     Composition is neat   _____ (possible 5 pts.)
     Grammar and Spelling   _____ (possible 5 pts.)

Subtotal Points _____ **(possible 83 pts.)**

Extra Credit
Word Puzzle   _____ (5 pt. per completed puzzle)
Complete an Enrichment Activity   _____ (possible 5 pts.)
Oral presentation   _____ (possible 10 pts.)

Total Extra Credit   _____

Total Unit Points _____

GRADE CHART

A   75-83+ points

B   67-74 points

C   59-66 points

D   51-58 points

Three members of the Black Wolf Squadron 1920 Alaska Air Expedition visit with young boy and his dog near a World War I bomber, an American De Havilland DH 4.

UNIT 8: DARING FLYBOYS

LESSON 24: EIELSON: ALASKA'S PIONEER AVIATOR

FACTS TO KNOW

Carl Benjamin Eielson – The pilot who flew the first commercial flight in Alaska
Commercial flight – For-profit flights to take passengers to a specific destination

COMPREHENSION QUESTIONS

1) Where was Carl Benjamin Eielson from? How did he end up in Alaska?

_____

_____

_____

_____

2) What was the first commercial airplane company in Alaska? Who formed the company? _____

_____

_____

3) Why did it take Carl Benjamin Eielson three times as long as it should have to get to Nenana ball field on his first flight there on July 4, 1923? _____

_____

_____

_____

4) Describe the first commercial flight in Alaska? How did this flight compare to the typical route from Fairbanks? _____

_____

_____

_____

5) How was Carl Benjamin Eielson involved in the start of airmail service in Alaska?

_____

_____

_____

_____

6) How did Carl Ben Eielson die at 32 years of age? _____

_____

_____

_____

DISCUSSION QUESTION

(Discuss this question with your teacher or write your answer in essay form below. Use additional paper if necessary.)

Do you think that there are as many plane crashes today as there were in the early 1900s? Why or why not?

_____

_____

_____

_____

_____

_____

_____

_____

_____

_____

_____

_____

_____

_____

_____

_____

ENRICHMENT ACTIVITY

Look for this book at your local library:
Wings Over Alaska: The Story of Carl Ben Eielson, Edward A. Herron. New York: Julian Messner, 1959.

Write a one-page book report on what you learned about his life. What were the most interesting parts of the biography to you?

LEARN MORE

Read more about Carl Ben Eielson by visiting https://www.britannica.com/biography/Carl-Ben-Eielson

UNIT 8: DARING FLYBOYS

LESSON 25: WIEN: A LEGEND IN THE NORTH

FACTS TO KNOW

Noel Wien – Famous pilot who founded Wien Air Alaska in the 1930s
Ralph Wien – Older brother of Noel who became director of Fairbanks Airplane
   Corporation
"Anchorage" (not the city) – The plane that Noel Wien flew in Anchorage

COMPREHENSION QUESTIONS

1) Describe the scene that *Anchorage Daily Times* reported when Anchorage residents
cleared land for their first airstrip. _____

_____

_____

_____

2) What historic flight did Noel Wien fly on July 15, 1924? What needed to be done to
prepare the plane for this flight? _____

_____

_____

_____

3) How did the historic flight referenced in Question #2 change the way that Alaskans
thought about transportation? _____

_____

_____

_____

4) Name at least one other way that Noel Wien made history. _____

_____

_____

_____

DISCUSSION QUESTION

(Discuss this question with your teacher or write your answer in essay form below. Use additional paper if necessary.)

How do you think modern life would be different without air travel?

_____
_____
_____
_____
_____
_____
_____
_____
_____
_____
_____
_____
_____
_____
_____

ENRICHMENT ACTIVITY

You have learned a lot about the history of aviation in Alaska over the last two units of this course. Create your own timeline of Alaska aviation history beginning with Professor Leonard's first venture into Alaska's skies in 1899.

LEARN MORE

Look for this book at your local library:
The Wien Brothers' Story, by Kay Kennedy. Fairbanks Alaska, 1967.

UNIT 8: DARING FLYBOYS

LESSON 26: MERRILL: BLAZING TRAILS IN THE SKY

FACTS TO KNOW

Russell Hyde Merrill – The first pilot to fly a commercial flight across the Arctic Circle

Anchorage Air Transportation – Aviation company that Russell Merrill flew for in the 1920s

COMPREHENSION QUESTIONS

1) What was the first commercial flight westward from Juneau and the first attempt by a single-engine plane to cross the Gulf of Alaska? _____

_____

_____

_____

2) Describe the flight that Russell Merrill and Noel Wien flew in 1928. How did Merrill almost die after the flight? _____

_____

_____

_____

3) What happened to Russell Merrill? What are some theories? _____

_____

_____

_____

4) How did the city of Anchorage honor Russell Merrill? _____

_____

_____

_____

DISCUSSION QUESTION

(Discuss this question with your teacher or write your answer in essay form below. Use additional paper if necessary.)

What legacy did aviators like Russell Hyde Merrill, Carl Benjamin Eielson and Noel Wien leave?

_____

_____

_____

_____

_____

_____

_____

_____

_____

_____

_____

_____

_____

_____

_____

LEARN MORE

Read more about pioneer aviator Russell Hyde Merrill by visiting:
http://www.alaskahistory.org/biographies/merrill-russel-hyde/

TIME TO REVIEW

Review Chapters 24-26 of your book before moving on the Unit Review. See how many questions you can answer without looking at your book.

UNIT 7: DARING FLYBOYS

REVIEW LESSONS 24-26

Write down what you remember about:

Carl Benjamin Eielson _____

_____

Commercial Flight _____

_____

Noel Wien _____

_____

Ralph Wien _____

_____

"Anchorage" (not the city) _____

_____

Russell Hyde Merrill _____

_____

Anchorage Air Transportation _____

_____

Fill in the blanks

1) _____ made news on July 16, 1923, when he flew the first _____ flight in Alaska. Not only did it cost the _____ $450 less for the plane ride compared to travel along the trail from _____, but it also saved time. The trail route took about six days, and the airplane trip took just _____.

2) In 1924, the _____ sent a De Havilland DH-4BM aircraft to Alaska for pilot _____ to use for experimental _____ runs between Nenana and McGrath.

3) James Rodebaugh hired _____ to make the first-ever flight between _____ and _____. This historic flight, which lasted just under _____, changed the way Alaskans thought about _____ forever. That same journey by _____ took two days.

4) To prepare for Noel Wien's historic flight, local mechanic Oscar Gill fabricated an auxiliary _____ for the craft. It allowed the plane to travel several hundred miles without needing to _____.

5) The summer of 1925 brought a milestone in Alaska aviation when two _____ wanted to travel from _____ to _____. _____ flew them to the village, located about 80 miles north of the _____, thus making the first flight across the _____.

6) _____ made his first appearance in Alaska when he flew from _____ to _____ in July 1925. In August, along with Roy Davis, he flew a Curtiss F Flying Boat to _____ in the first attempt by a single-engine plane to cross the _____. It was the first _____ air flight westward from Juneau, as well.

7) In May 1928, _____ had one of his most narrow brushes with death. It was on the first commercial flight to _____ for the Fox Film Expedition to Alaska to photograph _____ scenes to be used later in a screen story. _____ had the contract and needed another pilot.

8) A _____ found _____ snow blind, exhausted and unable to travel any farther on June 4, 1928. _____ said after he'd eaten all the food he'd brought with him, he'd killed _____ and eaten them raw. He recovered from his blindness while in the Barrow hospital, but he almost died from _____ spotted fever, caused by his diet of _____.

9) _____ city leaders approved a larger runway on the northern side of town, which later was named _____ in honor of _____.

UNIT 8: DARING FLYBOYS

Unit Test

Write at least three pragraphs about each of the three pioneer aviators that you studied in this unit. Be sure to include the following in your summation: What was this aviator most famous for? Describe one of his historic flights.

1) Carl Ben Eielson
2) Noel Wien
3) Russell Merrill

Use extra paper in back of the book if needed.

_____
_____
_____
_____
_____
_____
_____
_____
_____
_____
_____
_____
_____
_____
_____
_____
_____
_____
_____
_____
_____
_____
_____

UNIT 8: DARING FLYBOYS

Review Questions _____ (possible 7 pts.)
Fill-the-Blanks _____ (possible 9 pts.)

Unit Test

Essay 1
Demonstrates understanding of the topic _____ (possible 5 pts.)
Answered the questions completely and accurately _____ (possible 5 pts.)
Composition is neat _____ (possible 5 pts.)
Grammar and Spelling _____ (possible 5 pts.)

Essay 2
Demonstrates understanding of the topic _____ (possible 5 pts.)
Answered the questions completely and accurately _____ (possible 5 pts.)
Composition is neat _____ (possible 5 pts.)
Grammar and Spelling _____ (possible 5 pts.)

Essay 3
Demonstrates understanding of the topic _____ (possible 5 pts.)
Answered the questions completely and accurately _____ (possible 5 pts.)
Composition is neat _____ (possible 5 pts.)
Grammar and Spelling _____ (possible 5 pts.)

Subtotal Points _____ **(possible 76 pts.)**

Extra Credit

Word Puzzle _____ (5 pt. per completed puzzle)
Complete an Enrichment Activity _____ (possible 5 pts.)
Oral presentation _____ (possible 10 pts.)

Total Extra Credit _____

Total Unit Points _____

GRADE CHART

A   69-76+ points

B   61-68 points

C   53-60 points

D   45-52 points

Aviation Terms

Word Search Puzzle

Find the words listed below

```
N  N  Q  S  D  M  T  D  A  D  C  G  M  X  C  D  J  A  N  M
U  V  J  J  O  B  X  I  Z  I  N  I  M  Q  I  K  P  Y  Z  O
X  Y  I  A  T  G  B  V  P  Y  R  N  N  D  M  O  J  D  Z  T
I  C  E  Y  R  A  H  J  W  K  L  S  G  A  R  D  B  R  N  O
U  U  C  V  L  S  K  T  Q  U  C  I  P  T  H  R  Z  E  F  R
C  E  Y  C  R  F  V  E  D  X  N  O  O  E  F  C  F  T  I  N
E  K  J  I  L  U  N  G  O  Z  N  T  C  V  E  O  E  E  A  O
J  C  B  T  W  T  S  P  K  F  I  N  D  M  J  D  D  M  N  A
F  W  A  D  S  K  H  L  M  P  F  L  O  E  C  F  R  I  K  P
N  E  D  P  K  G  N  A  A  C  E  S  J  U  K  I  B  T  R  X
H  F  L  W  S  Q  Q  N  E  I  J  B  B  D  A  A  V  L  S  V
R  M  W  E  N  R  B  E  F  S  R  E  G  N  E  S  S  A  P  R
M  W  U  Q  O  H  I  R  Y  N  T  E  K  J  O  A  M  J  C  V
D  Z  L  H  O  S  I  A  W  U  Q  Y  A  P  H  T  D  I  Y  S
J  P  U  T  T  A  R  D  U  C  Y  A  S  E  W  A  W  T  W  M
E  S  A  B  N  C  Q  B  C  R  F  W  J  J  K  W  E  P  K  R
T  W  J  C  O  F  Q  N  N  Q  Z  N  L  A  N  D  I  N  G  S
B  E  J  Z  P  M  N  A  A  Z  C  U  E  Y  J  L  Z  N  N
X  G  P  S  Z  K  H  A  N  G  A  R  O  K  O  Z  N  B  B  F
R  C  S  V  N  R  O  T  A  I  V  A  P  T  T  I  M  Q  F  Q
```

AVIATOR	AIRSPEED	ALTIMETER
AIRSPACE	AERIALSURVEY	COCKPIT
MOTOR	PLANE	HANGAR
AIRMAN	MECHANIC	AIRFIELD
PILOT	PONTOONS	PASSENGERS
TAKEOFFS	LANDINGS	RUNWAY

UNIT 9: FROM THE NEWSROOM 1930s

LESSON 27: NATIVES GAIN RECOGNITION

FACTS TO KNOW

Indian Reorganization Act of 1935 – U.S. law that allowed American Indians to locally govern their affairs by tribal government

William Lewis Paul Sr. – Tlingit man who was the first Alaska Native to serve in the Territorial Legislature in 1924

Bureau of Indian Affairs – Branch of the federal government that administers land held in trust by the United States for American Indians, including Alaska Natives, and also is responsible for providing for their health care

COMPREHENSION QUESTIONS

1) Why weren't Alaska Natives allowed to become citizens after America purchased Alaska in 1867? _____

_____

_____

_____

2) What rights did the Indian Reorganization Act of 1935 afford Alaska Natives? (Be specific) _____

_____

_____

_____

3) When were Alaska Natives given the right to vote? What conditions had to be met?

_____

_____

_____

_____

4) What two milestones occurred in Alaska Native history in 1924? _____

_____

_____

_____

5) Describe the educational system for Native Alaskan children in the early 1900s.

_____

_____

_____

_____

DISCUSSION QUESTION

(Discuss this question with your teacher or write your answer in essay form below. Use additional paper if necessary.)

What do you think about the requirements placed upon Alaska Natives to dress in "western clothing" and speak only English?

_____

_____

_____

_____

_____

_____

_____

_____

_____

_____

_____

_____

_____

_____

_____

_____

ENRICHMENT ACTIVITY

Read the article at this link http://www.akhistorycourse.org/alaskas-cultures/tribal-governments-federal-law and then write a one-page summary about what you learned.

LEARN MORE

Tlingit Stories, by Maria Ackerman. Anchorage: Alaska Methodist University, 1975.

Read more about the Indian Reorganization Act and other important milestones in Alaska Native history by visiting http://www.akhistorycourse.org/governing-alaska/native-citizenship-and-land-issues

UNIT 9: FROM THE NEWSROOM 1930s

LESSON 28: COLONISTS SETTLE VALLEY

FACTS TO KNOW

Matanuska Valley – Area of southcentral Alaska known for agriculture

Col. Otto F. Ohlson – General Manager of the Alaska Railroad who helped start the Matanuska Valley Colony project

Great Depression of 1930s – The largest worldwide economic depression of the 20th century

The New Deal – A series of programs enacted by U.S. President Franklin D. Roosevelt to boost the economy between 1933-1939

COMPREHENSION QUESTIONS

1) Long before the _____ in _____ Alaska became one of the fastest-growing regions in the nation, _____ experimented in its fertile soil. They taught the _____ to grow crops like _____.

2) Why was the Matanuska Valley a good area for farming? _____
_____
_____
_____

3) How did the Great Depression of the 1930s jump-start the population growth of the Matanska Valley? _____
_____
_____
_____

4) When colonists arrived in Alaska as part of the Matanuska Valley Colony project, what did they receive? _____
_____
_____
_____

5) What was life like for the colonists? _____
_____
_____
_____

DISCUSSION QUESTION

(Discuss this question with your teacher or write your answer in essay form below. Use additional paper if necessary.)

How did Alaskans feel about the colonists who arrived in Alaska under the Matanuska Valley Colony project?

_____
_____
_____
_____
_____
_____
_____
_____
_____
_____
_____
_____
_____
_____
_____
_____
_____

ENRICHMENT ACTIVITY

Imagine that you are one of the colonists who relocated to the Matanuska Valley. Write a letter to a friend or family member about your adventures traveling to Alaska and settling in the valley.

LEARN MORE

Read more about farming history in Alaska by visiting http://www.akhistorycourse.org/americas-territory/alaskas-heritage/chapter-4-17-farming-herding-and-lumbering

UNIT 9: FROM THE NEWSROOM 1930s

LESSON 29: SOURDOUGH GOVERNOR APPOINTED

FACTS TO KNOW

John Weir Troy – Served as Alaska's 12th territorial governor from 1933-1939
University of Alaska – The first university in Alaska and was established at Fairbanks

COMPREHENSION QUESTIONS

1) Why did Alaskans heave a collective sigh of relief when John Troy was appointed the territory's 12th governor? _____

_____

_____

_____

2) What led John Troy to Alaska in 1897? What did he do for work when he got there?

_____

_____

_____

_____

3) What did John Troy believe was Alaska's greatest need? What did he think was needed in order to accomplish this? _____

_____

_____

_____

4) How was John Troy involved in boosting centers of learning in the territory?

_____

_____

_____

_____

DISCUSSION QUESTION

(Discuss this question with your teacher or write your answer in essay form below. Use additional paper if necessary.)

What did John Troy think about the Matanuska Valley Colony project?

_____
_____
_____
_____
_____
_____
_____
_____
_____
_____
_____
_____
_____
_____
_____
_____
_____

ENRICHMENT ACTIVITY

Watch this short YouTube video to learn more about the New Deal:
https://www.youtube.com/watch?v=U_FVa_Rx_ek

LEARN MORE

Read more about John Wier Troy by visiting http://www.juneau.org/library/museum/GCM/readarticle.php?UID=797&newxtkey=

UNIT 9: FROM THE NEWSROOM 1930s
LESSON 30: BLACK FOG OVER BARROW

FACTS TO KNOW

Will Rogers – Beloved humorist who died in a plane crash near Point Barrow in 1935

Wiley Post – The pilot of the plane who died along with Will Rogers when they crashed in 1935

Barrow – The farthest-north community in the United States near the area that Wiley Post and Will Rogers crashed and died; in 2016, the community voted for the town to retake its original name of Utqiaġvik

COMPREHENSION QUESTIONS

1) Why did Wiley Post want to fly to Alaska? Why did Will Rogers want to fly to Alaska?

_____

_____

_____

_____

2) What was Rogers' and Post's intended destination for the trip? _____

_____

_____

_____

_____

3) What warnings did the men receive about the flight to Barrow? _____

_____

_____

_____

4) Why did Post land in the water 12 miles away from Barrow? What did he and Rogers do when they landed there? _____

_____

_____

_____

5) What happened when Wiley Post and Will Rogers took off after landing on the water 12 miles from Barrow? _____

_____

_____

_____

DISCUSSION QUESTION

(Discuss this question with your teacher or write your answer in essay form below. Use additional paper if necessary.)

How was Will Rogers remembered after his death? What are some ways that he was honored after his death?

_____

_____

_____

_____

_____

_____

_____

_____

_____

_____

_____

_____

_____

_____

_____

LEARN MORE

Read more about Will Rogers by visiting http://www.willrogers.com/the-man

MAP ACTIVITY

Find the following places on the map where Will Rogers and Wiley Post traveled:
1) Juneau   2) Anchorage   3)Matanuska Valley   4) Fairbanks   5) Barrow

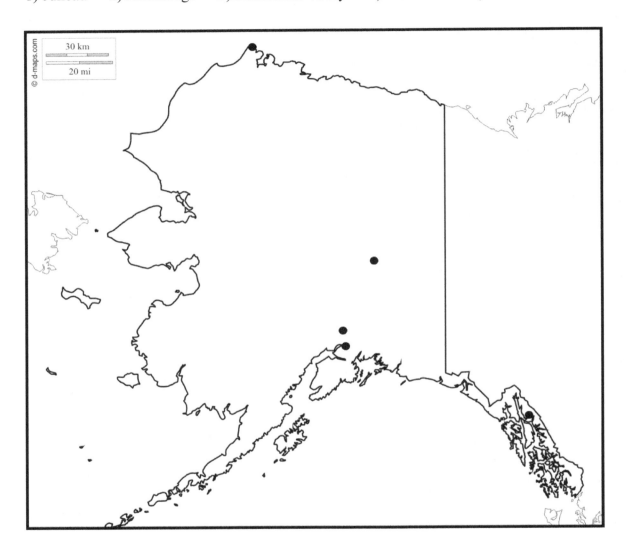

After getting lost in a fog, Wiley Post finally saw a lone reindeer herder, like this man, near a lagoon so he landed his plane to ask for directions to Barrow.

UNIT 9: FROM THE NEWSROOM 1930s

LESSON 31: OTHER NEWS AROUND ALASKA

Write 1-2 brief sentences summarizing each headline:

1) **Anchorage 1935 – First Fur Rendezvous Celebrated** _____
_____
_____
_____

2) **Bristol Bay 1935 – Salmon was King** _____
_____
_____
_____

3) **Fairbanks 1935 – Ice Carnival Created** _____
_____
_____
_____

4) **Juneau 1935 – Labor Strike Ends in Violence** _____
_____
_____

5) **Ketchikan 1935 – Alaska Sportsman Born** _____
_____
_____
_____

6) **Nome 1934 – Fire Destroys Downtown Businesses** _____
_____
_____
_____

7) Palmer 1936 – First Fair in the Valley _____

_____

_____

_____

8) Valdez 1932 – Aviator Reeve Arrived in Alaska _____

_____

_____

_____

LEARN MORE

Look for this book at your local library:
The Alaskans, by Wheeler, Keith. Alexandria, Virginia: Time-Life Books, 1977.

TIME TO REVIEW

Review Chapters 27-31 of your book before moving on the Unit Review. See how many questions you can answer without looking at your book.

UNIT 9: FROM THE NEWSROOM 1930s

REVIEW LESSONS 27-31

Write down what you remember about:

Reorganization Act of 1935 _____

_____

William Lewis Paul Sr. _____

_____

Bureau of Indian Affairs _____

_____

Matanuska Valley _____

_____

Col. Otto F. Ohlson _____

_____

Great Depression of 1930s _____

_____

The New Deal _____

_____

John Weir Troy _____

_____

University of Alaska _____

_____

Will Rogers _____

_____

Wiley Post _____

_____

Barrow _____

_____

Fill in the blanks:

1) Amended in _____ to include Alaska, the _____ allowed American Indians to locally govern their affairs by a _____ government that was established by constitution and bylaws for each tribe.

2) It took years of hard work, but Alaska Natives were given the right to _____ in 1922. However, certain _____ had to be met such as: wear _____; not _____ or speak _____; and live apart from _____.

3) _____, general manager of the Alaska Railroad since 1928, also had been trying to entice _____ to the _____ in an effort to spur railbelt settlement toward Palmer. But despite the area's _____ valleys and abundant sources of fresh water, settlers didn't stream into the area.

4) _____ helped the Department of Interior and the Federal Emergency Rehabilitation Administration plan a _____community, and U.S. President _____ approved the project known as the _____ Colony in his New Deal in 1935.

5) The _____ under the _____ Colony project drew lots for 40 acres and a homestead, a deal that included a _____. They also received _____ for $_____ at 3 percent interest to pay for it all. In addition, each family was given temporary _____, a _____ allowance of $75, medical care and help clearing the land and building a _____.

6) _____ served as Alaska's 12th territorial governor from 1933-1939. He was a firm believer that the territory should become a _____. And Troy thought a larger _____ and a better _____ system would help achieve that goal.

7) _____ also believed in boosting centers of _____ in the territory. In 1935, he signed the _____ that changed the name of the college in Fairbanks and started the illustrious _____.

8) _____ of _____ became the first Alaska Native to graduate from the _____ in Fairbanks in 1935.

9) Aviator _____ invited humorist _____ to travel to Alaska and beyond with him in 1935. Their plans were vague when they took off from Seattle early in August for the "Roof of the World," _____.

10) On learning that _____ was only 12 miles away, the adventurers returned to the plane and took off. According to an Eskimo named _____, everything seemed to go all right until they were up about 400 or 500 feet. Then suddenly their _____. The plane went into a _____, hitting the shallow lagoon with the speed of a rocket and _____ so that engine and fuselage were buried under three feet of water.

Greetings from Fairbanks, Alaska
Season's Best Wishes

This postcard illustrates the talent of ice carvers in Fairbanks, home of the Ice Carnival.

From the Newsroom 1930s

Crossword Puzzle

Read Across and Down clues and fill in blank boxes that match numbers on the clues

Across

4 Town that sometimes is called "the top of the world"
9 Last name of reindeer herder who gave men directions before fatal crash in 1935
10 The new Southcentral farmers' community received 18 miles of netting to battle this pest in 1935
11 Name of steamship that carried first group of farmers to Alaska in 1935
12 Aviation pioneer who crashed and died near "the top of the world" in 1935
13 Alaska governor from 1933-1939
15 Alaska Natives were not considered this when Alaska became part of the United States in 1867
18 Government minted tokens that farmers used as currency in 1935
19 This swept through Nome in 1934, and Seward in 1935, and destroyed most of their downtown areas
23 Name for an old-timer in Alaska
25 A procession of people or vehicles moving through a public place
28 Will Rogers' hometown in Oklahoma
30 Name of pilot who carried two bodies from "the top of the world" back to the States
32 This arrived in the Southcentral Alaska farmers' community long before farmers could use it in 1935
34 Rex Beach said that Alaska summer weather can be this
36 Sometimes called "farmers of the sea"
37 The people who taught Alaska Natives to grow crops in the 1800s
38 What the farmers who came to Southcentral Alaska in 1935 were called
39 Reason airplane got lost heading to "the top of the world" in 1935
40 An institution of higher learning
41 Valley where farmers from Midwestern and Northern states settled in 1935 to begin farming
42 Alaska Natives were given the right to do this (under certain conditions) in 1922
43 Structures farmers first lived in when they arrived to build an agricultural community in 1935

Down

1 Type of body of water that Rogers' plane crashed into before fatal 1935 crash
2 Much-loved humorist who traveled to Alaska in 1935 and then died in an airplane crash
3 The U.S. government sent 150 horses to the new Southcentral Alaska farmers' community but forgot to send any of these in 1935
5 Game played at the first Ice Carnival in Fairbanks
6 Renewable resource that was king in the 1930s
7 A person's or family's residence, which comprises the land, house and outbuildings
8 Name of schooner that stalled on a sandbar near Ugashik Bay in 1935
13 Alaska Natives were given authority to have this type of government under the Indian Reorganization Act of 1935
14 First Alaska Native to graduate from the University of Alaska Fairbanks in 1935
16 Reason that first group of farmers were quarantined on the steamship for a week when they arrived in Seward in April 1935
17 Aviator who arrived in Valdez in 1932 and later built one of Alaska's best-known airways
20 Southeast town where labor unrest occurred in May 1935

From the Newsroom 1930s
Crossword Puzzle

Down (Continued)

21 Town in Matanuska Valley where the first fair was held in 1936
22 Tough economic times are called this
24 Name of celebration that began in Anchorage in 1935 that centered around furs
26 Some, including governor during 1933-1939, thought more of this would help Alaska become a state
27 Woman crowned this at Fairbanks Ice Festival
29 U.S. President who created the New Deal programs during the 1930s
31 Name of publication born in 1935 that later became known as the *Alaska Magazine*
33 William Lewis Paul Sr., the first Alaska Native to serve in Alaska's Territorial Legislature, belonged to this Native group
35 He was general manager of the Alaska Railroad and tried to get farmers interested in agriculture during the late 1920s-early 1930s

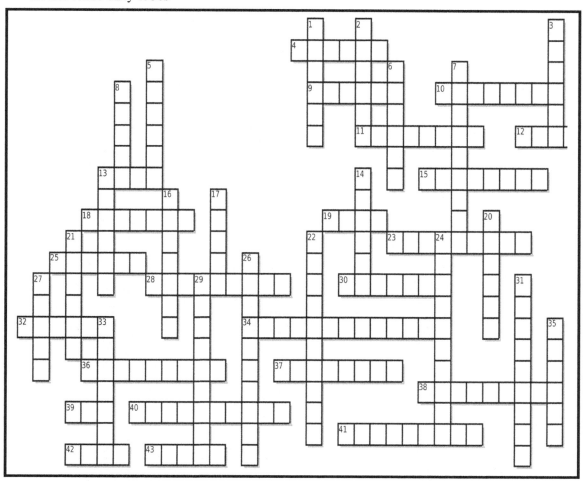

UNIT 9: FROM THE NEWSROOM 1930s

Unit Test

Choose *three* of the following questions to answer in paragraph form. Use as much detail as possible to completely answer the question. Use extra paper in back of the book if needed.

1) Why weren't Alaska Natives considered citizens when the United States purchased Alaska in 1867? What kind of requirements did Alaska Natives need to meet in order to vote in 1922?

2) What was the purpose of the Matanuska Valley Colony project? How did it benefit the colonists? How did it benefit Alaska?

3) Name two major things that John Weir Troy accomplished while serving as Alaska's 12th territorial governor from 1933-1939.

4) Describe what happened when Wiley Post and Will Rogers took a trip to Alaska.

UNIT 9: FROM THE NEWSROOM 1930s

Review Questions	_____	(possible 12 pts.)
Fill-the-Blanks	_____	(possible 10 pts.)

Unit Test

Essay 1

Demonstrates understanding of the topic	_____	(possible 5 pts.)
Answered the questions completely and accurately	_____	(possible 5 pts.)
Composition is neat	_____	(possible 5 pts.)
Grammar and Spelling	_____	(possible 5 pts.)

Essay 2

Demonstrates understanding of the topic	_____	(possible 5 pts.)
Answered the questions completely and accurately	_____	(possible 5 pts.)
Composition is neat	_____	(possible 5 pts.)
Grammar and Spelling	_____	(possible 5 pts.)

Essay 3

Demonstrates understanding of the topic	_____	(possible 5 pts.)
Answered the questions completely and accurately	_____	(possible 5 pts.)
Composition is neat	_____	(possible 5 pts.)
Grammar and Spelling	_____	(possible 5 pts.)

Subtotal Points _____ **(possible 82 pts.)**

Extra Credit

Word Puzzle	_____	(5 pt. per completed puzzle)
Complete an Enrichment Activity	_____	(possible 5 pts.)
Oral presentation	_____	(possible 10 pts.)

Total Extra Credit _____

Total Unit Points _____

GRADE CHART

A   75-82+ points

B   67-74 points

C   59-66 points

D   51-58 points

EXTRA PAPER FOR LESSONS

EXTRA PAPER FOR LESSONS

EXTRA PAPER FOR LESSONS

EXTRA PAPER FOR LESSONS

EXTRA PAPER FOR LESSONS

EXTRA PAPER FOR LESSONS

EXTRA PAPER FOR LESSONS

EXTRA PAPER FOR LESSONS

EXTRA PAPER FOR LESSONS